The Middle Eastern Vegetarian Cookbook

Salma Hage

The Middle Eastern Vegetarian Cookbook

Salma Hage

Acknowledgment

I dedicate this book to my grandson George. I'd like to thank my son Joe, first and foremost, for making this possible and I'd also like to extend my gratitude to Lucie, Jess, and Alain for their contributions. And lastly, thank you to Emilia, Michelle, Matt, Lucy, Liz, Max, and our dedicated testers for their involvement in the book.

Phaidon Press Limited
Regent's Wharf
All Saints Street
London N1 9PA

Phaidon Press Inc.
65 Bleecker Street
New York, NY 10012

phaidon.com

First published 2016
© 2016 Phaidon Press Limited

ISBN: 978 0 7148 7130 1

A CIP catalogue record for this book is available from the British Library.

Commissioning Editor: Emilia Terragni
Project Editor: Michelle Meade
Production Controller: Amanda Mackie
Designer: Aaron Garza
Photographers: Liz and Max Haarala Hamilton

Printed in China

The publisher would like to thank Joe Hage, Lena Hall, Lizzie Harris, Jess Lea-Wilson, Lucy Malouf, Pene Parker, Susan Spaull, Dara Sutin, and Lucie Ware for their contributions to the book.

Recipe Notes

Butter should always be unsalted.

Unless otherwise stated, all herbs are fresh and parsley is flat-leaf parsley.

Pepper is always freshly ground black pepper, unless otherwise specified.

Eggs, vegetables, and fruits are assumed to be large (UK: medium) size, unless otherwise specified.

Milk is always full-fat (whole), unless otherwise specified.

Garlic cloves are assumed to be large; use two if small.

Cooking and preparation times are for guidance only, as individual ovens vary. If using a fan (convection) oven, follow the manufacturer's instructions concerning oven temperatures.

Some of the recipes require advanced techniques, specialist equipment, and professional experience to achieve good results.

To test whether your deep-frying oil is hot enough, add a cube of stale bread. If it browns in thirty seconds, the temperature is 350–375°F (180–190°C), about right for most frying. Exercise a high level of caution when following recipes involving any potentially hazardous activity, including the use of high temperature and open flames. In particular, when deep-frying, add the food carefully to avoid splashing, wear long sleeves, and never leave the pan unattended.

Some recipes include raw or very lightly cooked eggs. These should be avoided particularly by the elderly, infants, pregnant women, convalescents, and anyone with an impaired immune system.

Both metric and imperial measures are used in this book. Follow one set of measurements throughout, not a mixture, as they are not interchangeable.

All spoon measurements are level.
1 teaspoon = 5 ml; 1 tablespoon = 15 ml. Australian standard tablespoons are 20 ml, so Australian readers are advised to use 3 teaspoons in place of 1 tablespoon when measuring small quantities.

When no quantity is specified, for example of oils, salts, and herbs used for finishing dishes, quantities are discretionary and flexible.

Cooking Bonds

Cooking builds invisible yet strong links between people, countries, and epochs. When Salma tells us about her first culinary experiences, I feel like nodding and saying: "I know so well what you mean!" I also had a grandmother to whom I owe my early interest in cooking. The two stories, hers and mine, took place at a distance of more than 1,850 miles (3,000 kilometers), with an interval of some years. Each of them has its own parameters, different cultural environments, and obviously, genders—yet Salma's personal story resonates very profoundly with my own relationship with cooking.

I was born and grew up in a farm in southwest France. My grandmother used to cook for the whole family and her recipes left an unforgettable imprint in my mind. For instance, I can still today remember the smell and taste of the roasted chicken she often prepared for Sunday lunches. The scent of the poultry slowly roasting in the oven pervaded easily—and very pleasantly—to my bedroom, which was located just above the kitchen. Her classic dish represents the pure and simple perfection of what a roasted chicken must be.

Even more important, I learned from her something absolutely crucial: before cooking, there is nature. My grandmother didn't teach me this lesson with long and wordy discourses; the message went through from practice—which is sometimes much more effective for a young and turbulent kid like I was. It always started with this innocent question: What are we going to eat today? And my grandmother's answer was invariably: Go to the kitchen garden and pick the ripe vegetables. This is the simplest and clearest way of understanding that it is up to nature to decide what we should eat.

Aside from the sacrosanct Sunday roasted chicken, meat had a modest role in our daily diet. The family was not vegan in the modern sense; for instance, vegetables were usually prepared with a piece of lard. Yet, partly by choice and partly because of economic constraints, meat was not seen as being necessarily the center of the meals.

Would it be only this childhood experience, Salma and myself would already share a lot in the molding of our respective food habits. And this would be sufficient to explain why her book moves me so much—because it conjures up such intimate memories for me.

As years passed, I began to realize my sole and dearest ambition: to become a cook. And then happened what proves to be probably one of the most crucial events in my professional life: I discovered Mediterranean cuisine. Or rather, I discovered the Mediterranean civilization, because its food is so intrinsically linked with the soil, the peoples, their history, and ways of life. This encounter took place on the French and Italian Rivieras, this strip of land starting approximately from the Îles d'Hyères, in France, and finishing after Genoa, with the Ligurian Sea, in Italy.

I fell in love with the Rivieras. I got to know this region, wandering around to admire the landscapes, hunting the best market gardeners or stockbreeders, arriving on the piers at dawn to get the catch from small fishermen, haunting the open air markets to listen to women disclosing ancient recipes. All this gave birth to my own interpretation of the Mediterranean cuisine I developed for Le Louis XV, my Monaco restaurant. Since then, my passion for the Mediterranean cuisine never been exhausted.

Reading Salma's book, I feel an intense sentiment of familiarity. United by the Mediterranean Sea, we look at the same picture, each of us from our opposite ends of our common sea. We love the same tastes, the same traditions, the same values. I dare to say we convey the same, fundamental message: The Mediterranean cuisine, this very ancient tradition, is incredibly modern.

Emphasizing the long history of the Mediterranean and Middle Eastern cuisine, the depth of theirs roots, is the guarantee of their vitality. The Mediterranean—which not only encompasses Italy, France, and Greece to the west, but also Turkey, Lebanon, and Palestine to the east—has some of the most vivid and inspiring contemporary cuisines.

When it comes to food, what issues are we confronted with? How to produce sufficient food for all the inhabitants of the planet without exploiting it? How to eat more healthily? In fact, these questions are the two faces of the same coin. Agriculture, rearing, and fishing techniques have to become sustainable to ensure the future of the planet and, at the same time, they must offer consumers products which are equally better to eat and better for their health. From all these viewpoints, the Mediterranean cuisine suggests a virtuous pattern.

You'll start reading this book for the pleasure of browsing beautiful pages of superb meals. Then, you'll execute the recipes, enchant your taste buds, and discover a realm of new tastes and flavors. And, gradually, you'll change your views on your eating habits, searching for products that are better because they are soundly produced and fully satisfying recipes based on vegetables and grains.

You will step into the delicious world of contemporary Middle Eastern cuisine.

ALAIN DUCASSE

A New Way of Eating

A few months ago I received an email from a lady named Marianne. She'd picked up a copy of my first book—*The Lebanese Kitchen*— in a Chicago bookstore and wondered whether we might be related. She had a grandmother who was also called Salma and who was from the same village as me, Apple Hamlet. It turned out she was talking about my father's aunt—I was named after her—and Marianne was actually my father's cousin's daughter. Her grandmother used to visit my father in his tiny village in the mountains of Lebanon. So there we were: she in a bookstore in Chicago, me in my kitchen in London, and both of us connected to a tiny village of two hundred inhabitants in Lebanon! We have since become friends, and all because of a cookbook.

It was my father who encouraged me to cook. I was nine years old when I first made him *m'juderah* (page 208), a dish of lentils cooked with rice and covered in fried onions. He said, "My darling, that's delicious, you are such a lovely cook!" I am not sure how truthful he was being, but I believed him at the time and there began my love of cooking.

It was around that time I started to help my mom in the kitchen. We were a big family (mom had just given birth to her twelfth child) and, to be honest, being the eldest, I didn't have much choice but to become a kind of a second mom to them all. I would watch my mother and grandmother like a hawk, trying to learn as many recipes as I possibly could. *What spices go next? How much? Just a little more?* Back then, nothing was ever written down and nobody owned recipe books. When I first met my husband Heni, I used the cooking skills I had picked up as a means of impressing him. When my son Joe was born, my grandma came to live with us in an apartment we were renting in Tripoli, Lebanon, and she carried on teaching me new recipes to cook. For me, food and family will always be tied.

It has been five years since my first cookbook was published. It is funny to think that my recipes, some of which are our everyday family and village dishes, can now be found in bookstores around the world. I have received so many phone calls, letters, and emails since it was published—I often find it hard to believe how many people, from different countries and backgrounds, are enjoying these traditional Middle Eastern recipes.

Over the last four years, however, my cooking has changed significantly. My son Joe and my grandson George cut out the meat and fish from their diets and I wanted to continue preparing delicious, healthy, and satisfying meals for them, but admittedly, I felt perplexed. I used to really love making all of those dishes so it was a big upheaval to cut out meat and fish from my home-cooking and cook only with fruits, vegetables, legumes (pulses), and grains. At one point Heni, who

is now 84, said, "Here, take some money. Go and buy some meat!"
I replied, "I have money, I just don't like to cook meat anymore."
Of course, Heni still associates not having meat with being poor.

VEGETARIANISM AND VILLAGE LIFE

My brother said to me last week, "We were all much healthier when there wasn't so much food around." And, thinking about it, he was probably right.

For the first two or three decades of my life, as it had been for many earlier generations, my diet was mostly vegetarian. During and after the World War II, you would eat whatever you could lay your hands on and you would just thank God that you had food at all. By the 1960s, the variety of food available had increased a lot, but we still weren't really eating much meat and we didn't feel that we were missing anything.

The things we ate the most were beans, eggplants (aubergines), rice, lentils, and other legumes. For breakfast we would eat olives and white cheese such as feta. And we'd eat Manoushe breads (page 60) covered in Za'atar (page 27) made from thyme leaves that had been laid out to dry in the sunshine. We'd go around to the house where my mother baked her bread and, as it came out of the oven, we'd drizzle on a little olive oil and salt, roll it up around the olives and cheese, and eat it right there and then.

My mother used to make the dough at home, but because she never had her own bread oven, she used to go around to one of the neighbors. For every ten loaves that my mother baked in her oven, she would give the lady one loaf to keep as a kind of payment for using her oven. Other neighbors would come around to use the oven, too, so that lady never needed to make her own bread.

There was a small mill in the village that we would sometimes go to for flour, but I only remember going by myself a few times because I couldn't carry very much. My mother needed around fifty-five pounds (twenty-five kilograms) of flour each week, which was far more than I could carry, so my father would have to make a special trip into the local town to buy huge sacks of it.

Fifty-five pounds of flour every week meant a lot of kneading. On this scale, it becomes a very physical job and so my elder brothers had to all help out. After kneading, they put the dough into a large copper pan to rise and, once it had doubled in size, it was ready to bake. We would all cut and roll the bread into rounds and stretch it out on a *kara*—a kind of cushion. Our neighbor would take the rounds and stick them onto the sides of her clay oven, with the wood burning below. It would only take a few seconds before they'd be ready for her to pull them out. It was quite a large clay oven so she could bake around four huge flatbreads at a time, and as soon as she finished one batch she would put the next lot in. We would have bread to eat with most of our meals; sometimes we would just drizzle on olive oil and add a little salt, and, for a treat on a rare occasion, we'd sprinkle on some sugar.

Back then we pretty much ate what we could grow ourselves: figs, grapes, plums, peaches, apples, potatoes, onions, olives ... you name it. Everybody would grow what they could on their own land but, if a neighbor's figs didn't grow so well one year, we'd give them some of ours. We would swap whatever we had. In a small village such as ours, everybody helped each other out. If someone was getting married, the whole village would come together to help out. If there was a funeral, everyone would pull together. It was the same for any event.

It's true that meat and fish did feature in village life, but this was very rare. We didn't eat much meat at all, because we simply couldn't afford it. We used to keep some animals—my grandmother used to keep hens for example—but she would only use them for eggs to make dishes such as *Iijeh* (page 76), which are omelets made with the flesh of white Lebanese zucchini (courgettes). There was an archway behind our house through which people used to enter, and we used to place an egg there so the hens knew that's where they had to lay their eggs. We used to be so eager to make the *iijeh* that we would steal the eggs the hens were sitting on and replace them with a white onion. They used to fall for it every time and carry on laying eggs next to the onion. We were so short of food and pretty desperate back then.

As children, we always had an awareness of the value and significance of meat. It was forbidden to eat meat during lent, of course, so we also understood about abstaining from it. Meat was only really important during religious festivals. For instance, harisa is traditionally a meat dish that was only eaten on saint days. (I have included a recipe for a vegan version [page 79] that is a breakfast porridge made with cinnamon-spiced barley.) Every village had their own saint's day and everyone from the neighboring villages would bring along saucepans full of barley and cook the same dish in one big copper pot—a *tadissit*. Traditionally, half a dozen men would stir the pot with large wooden paddles throughout the night. While cooking, they would add in some cinnamon wood and, just before it was ready to serve, they would add quite a lot of cumin and give it another good stir. That's what made it special: all that effort and preparation. On the night of the celebrations, people would come with drums and play them for everyone to dance to. People would hold each other by the arms and dance together until late into the night, while somebody played the flute.

For what we couldn't grow or make ourselves, there was a small store. We could buy a few ounces of rice or sugar there, for example, but that was all. If, and when, we had some money, we would go to the big stores and markets in Tripoli, which was twelve miles (twenty

kilometers) away. There weren't many cars in my day—I even remember
a time when there weren't any cars at all—although there were taxi-
buses that went between the villages and towns. But you had to walk
up to another village in the mountains over a mile away to get one.
Heni's village, Sebhel, had a taxi service and these were the main two
connections into town for the markets and the souks. If we wanted
to go shopping, or to go the doctor, or wherever, we'd have to walk to
another village. When the first car arrived in our village in the early
1950s, everybody wanted to ride in it. How many people do you usually
fit in a car? Four or six people maybe? Well, the owner of this car used
to fit twenty people in every time he drove into town. People were on
the roof, in the trunk (boot), hanging out of the windows.

Fortunately, we have four seasons in Lebanon—and you really know
where you are with the seasons there. In the summer there is not a
drop of rain; it's very hot all the time. The season I like the most is spring,
because it's sunny, but not as hot, and you have regular rain showers,
so there's always plenty of water. There are also rain showers during
fall (autumn), but in winter we have snow and frost on the mountains.
Some people can't believe it gets so cold during winter. I remember
that my grandmother used to get someone to chop wooden logs for her
from the forest, and she'd fill half an entire room with them to get
through the winter. But the snow and ice from the mountains meant
that there was always some water available for most of the year.

I remember the soil being so hot during the summer—great for
growing things in—and we used it as an opportunity to stock up for
winter. We would plant onions and potatoes and after harvesting we'd dry
them outside in the sun so they lasted the whole winter. You wouldn't
expect potatoes to stay good for very long in such a hot climate, but
they do. And they'd go such a long way, too. Jidi ("grandfather") Potatoes
(page 167) was one of our favorite dishes of potatoes cooked simply with
onions and fresh mint. We'd also add them to soups, such as the Green
Split Pea Soup (page 191), which gives it a great texture. And, of course,
we made the best crisp fries! We would cut the potatoes into sticks, part-
fry them, and let them stand until we were ready to eat. Then we'd fry
them again quickly a second time and eat them dipped in garlicky oil.

We used to grow a lot of beans, too, and would use a needle and
thread to sew them together and hang them up to dry. Then, during the
winter, if we wanted some beans, we'd just take some down, put them
in boiling water, and they'd come up nice and fresh again.

I still keep the giant pots in our cellar in which my family used
to store olive oil to last us through the winter months. They were so
precious that there were specially made holes in the floor to stand them
in so that they wouldn't fall over. People often use the pots decoratively
these days, but I remember when they were essential.

We would also pickle a lot of different ingredients too, which was another way of preserving produce. We used to pickle cucumbers, onions, and eggplants (aubergines) and all kinds of vegetables. Turnips were one of the favorites to pickle, and it's so easy to do. You wash the turnips, slice them up, and salt them. Then, you boil them in water and let them cool. Finally, you put them in a jar with equal measures of distilled water and vinegar. To make them a nice red color, the trick is to add some beets (beetroots) to the jar, then screw the lid on tight—and a few weeks later they are ready to eat. They never last long. I can never throw any jars away even to this day. In fact, my family laughs at me now because I have a hard time throwing anything away at all.

Tomato Paste (Puree) (page 27) was another great preserve we made for the winter, and I remember that my grandma used to love to spread it on top of flatbread. I still make it when I'm over in Lebanon and bring it back to England. It's so much nicer than the tomato paste you get from a store but requires a lot more effort. You slice the tomatoes, boil them, and put them through a strainer (sieve) to get rid of all the seeds. When I was a child, we made it in huge quantities and stayed up all night to boil and stir the pots. A dish we made with the help of the sunshine was *kishik*, which is a mix of bulgur wheat and yogurt. We'd stir them together, put the mix out in the sunshine and, when it was dry, grind it up like a powder. Even nowadays I sometimes use kishik powder to make a soup for Heni's breakfast. I fry some garlic and stir in half a cup of kishik and half a cup of water and he eats it with big chunks of thickly sliced bread for dunking.

So much has changed, of course, and the arrival of supermarkets and better transport has meant that villagers have access to most of the things that the modern world has to offer today. And, as with our family, many people spend time living and working in other larger towns, cities, and different countries, so village life is very different to what it once was. But whenever I return to Apple Hamlet, I am pleased to see so many of the traditional ways of preparing food still being practiced today, with many of the old recipes as popular as ever.

THE MIDDLE EASTERN VEGETARIAN COOKBOOK

"Don't spill that water!" my grandmother used to shout. It seems funny now, but back then there was no running water in our home, only two faucets (taps) at either end of the village. My grandmother used to put handles on large buckets and I had to go back and forth to fill them up. Back and forth, back and forth. My arms ached so much. Nowadays, my son laughs at me for recycling water bottles by filling them with tap water and stacking them in the refrigerator. He thinks I am trying to trick people into thinking it's bottled water, but the truth is that those long journeys to and from the faucets have never left me.

I learned a lot from my grandma while she was living with me in Tripoli. One very simple trick was how to cook an eggplant over a naked flame. Once it was nice and soft, we would peel away the charred skin, mash the flesh up with garlic, salt, and olive oil (no tahini), and eat it with bread. We call it "Grandma's Eggplant Dip" (page 109). She would always cook with a clay pot on the wood fire and made simple things, such as green beans with onions and garlic. That was a meal for us back then, not a side dish. She'd make lentils and rice, or beans and rice in that same clay pot and it always used to taste so delicious. In this book, I've included my version of her recipes, such as Chickpea and Rice M'juderah (page 215) and Rishta (page 212).

Some of the recipes in this book are traditional Lebanese dishes that are vegetarian and vegan anyway, but others are adapted from traditional meat dishes. To make tasty vegan dishes, you have to be inventive. You have to try things out. One of the traditional vegan dishes that Heni loves are stuffed grape (vine) leaves (page 184)—we call them *wara'inib* in Arabic—and he could eat them every day. I have a wonderful grape vine here in my London garden and I make them throughout the summer. After blanching the grape leaves quickly (just in and out), I roll them up around an herbed tomato-rice stuffing and pack them into a pan like cigars, where they simmer under a plate until the rice is cooked. They are just wonderful and sometimes I even give them to Heni as a special treat for breakfast, instead of the usual cheese, olives, and eggs. He always asks for more at lunchtime. We make a similar recipe using cabbage leaves and I've also included some other stuffed vegetable recipes, such as Quinoa Stuffed Peppers (page 148) and Stuffed Baby Eggplant (page 178).

Mezze dishes are a very important part of Middle Eastern cuisine and many of the most celebrated dishes are vegan. I've also included an Almond Hummus (page 93) and a Butternut Hummus (page 93) to add to the classic chickpea versions. Another equally delicious mezze is *Muhammara* (page 96), which I make with parsley, walnuts, and crisp bread crumbs so it comes out a little crunchy. I also add pomegranate molasses to *muhammara*, which gives it a lovely flavor, somewhere between sweet and sour. Sometimes people in the village make pomegranate molasses from fresh juice and I always try to bring a bottle back with me. *Muhammara* is great to serve alongside hummus and baba ganoush with warm flatbread—and if you have all three of them, you might not make it to the main course.

I wanted to include a vegan version of another famous mezze staple, kibbeh, which is often made with lamb—so instead, I have a recipe for Chickpea Kibbeh (page 115). The texture is very similar to meat kibbeh, but to get the bulgur wheat to bind, I discovered that you need to add some potato with the spices and herbs before baking it in a tray in the oven. You can also make a burger version from this mix, which I fry. Experimenting with the potato made me think about whether sweet potato might also work, and so then I came up with Little Damascus Kibbeh with Pine Nuts (page 112).

Falafel go down even faster than stuffed grape leaves in my house, so I have several recipes in this book including one which uses fava (broad) beans and mint (page 106); another version with a wonderful sesame coating (page 94), which are nice and crispy; and a recipe with bulgur (page 224). The best way to eat falafel, of course, is stuffed into flatbread with tomato, cucumber, and gherkins with a spoonful of Tahini (page 24).

In the Salads chapter, I have two twists on the classic tabbouleh (page 159 and 192) and a traditional recipe for the iconic Fattoush (page 137) as these are salads that I never tire of eating. I am especially excited about the Beets with Lebneh and Mint (page 118) and the Freekeh, Pomegranate, and Feta Salad (page 126). Freekeh is a kind of green wheat, harvested just before it's ripe. It has quite a nutty flavor and you can use it for sweet dishes, too. My father-in-law used to eat wheat or barley cereal every single morning, which he'd boil and eat before he went out to work. He had a book that said that if you eat barley you'll live for a hundred years—and it's certainly true that a lot of Lebanese people live to a great age.

One of my favorite dessert recipes in this book is for Tahini and Pomegranate Cookies (page 252)—they look like they have been studded with red jewels. I have included traditional recipes for Halva (page 256), a nutty, honeyed fudge, and the famous Lebanese celebratory cookies called Ma'mool Cookies (page 250), which I make in vast quantities around Christmas time.

I have also adapted a couple of very old desserts, including Meghli (page 268), which we make just after a mother gives birth. This is a kind of rice pudding, and you can eat it either as a sweet dessert or for breakfast.

And there are plenty of other ideas for breakfasts in the book, too, from savory *Mashlouka* (page 67), which is a dish of eggs cooked with potatoes and tomatoes, to sweet treats such as Ataif (page 64), which are rosewater pancakes served with ground pistachios and honey. When they were little, my grandchildren used to want pancakes all the time; they used to smile like little angels and beg me to make some. They reminded me so much of my own childhood, and how much we loved to add syrup and molasses to our pancakes. Sometimes we'd have sticky black carob molasses, but the one I loved best was made from grapes. I remember one memorable time when my father, who was a carpenter at the time, told us that he would be bringing some grape molasses home (sometimes people who didn't have much money would pay him with food). My brother and I were so excited that we couldn't sleep. We waited and waited for my father to come home, but in the end we fell asleep. The next morning we woke up and saw it there in the middle of the room—a copper pot with a handle and full of our beloved molasses.

Although my father was a carpenter, he always dreamed of becoming a priest. In 1956, there was a shortage of priests in the Middle East and the Pope gave special permission for anyone who wanted to become a priest to do so. One day at work, the man my father was making doors for asked him, "Why do you arrive at my house late every day?" My father replied, "It's because first I go to church every morning to attend mass."

"Why don't you become a priest?" said the man. And my father replied, "It is the only thing I have longed to be all my life."

"So why don't you train to become one then?" asked the man. But my father replied, "Because I don't have the money for the fees."

The man said to him, "You must go and I will pay the fees!"

So my father went to the seminary and he studied for two years to become a priest. During this time, his uncle and aunt helped my mother and us children to get by and when my father was ordained—it was the happiest day of his life. From then on, I used to watch him each week saying mass at the altar, just to see the pure joy in his face at doing what he loved the most in life. Every day, for the rest of his life, he said a prayer for the man who had paid for his fees to train as a priest.

For me, along with my family, cooking is the thing I love most in life. I never imagined that most of the meals I cook would become almost completely vegan, and totally vegetarian. In fact, you will see these two symbols throughout the book: Ⓥ for vegan-friendly and Ⓖ for gluten-free. Every kitchen has a set of pantry staples and mine is no exception. I usually prepare these at home, because I find that you can really taste the difference, and that there is something satisfying about making them yourself. You will find these recipes on pages 24–27, but if you're short on time, you can purchase them in Middle Eastern grocers or some larger supermarkets.

I love this new way of eating. I hope that you'll enjoy this new book of vegetarian and vegan recipes as much as I have enjoyed making it.

SALMA HAGE, LONDON

Glossary

AGAVE NECTAR/SYRUP
A sweetener made from the agave plant, the same plant as tequila and one-and-a-half times sweeter than sugar. It's ideal for sweetening hot beverages or used as a substitute for honey in baking.

ALLSPICE
Known also as Jamaican pepper or pimenta, this spice is indispensable in the Middle East and is often used to season stews and meats. It is available whole or ground.

ALMOND EXTRACT
A nut extract that is popular in baking. It is strong, sweet, clear and pure in flavor.

ALMONDS
A popular nut used to accent savory and sweet dishes. If a recipe calls for blanched almonds, simply soak whole nuts in boiled water for 15 minutes and drain. Press them between your fingers to remove the skins.

ANISE
Sweet and aromatic, anise has a strong licorice-like flavor and aroma and belongs to the family of plants that includes carrots, caraway, cumin, dill, fennel, and cilantro (coriander).

ARAK
This clear, colorless alcoholic drink from the Middle East has an anise flavor and makes a refreshing aperitif when combined with water and ice.

ATAIF
Sweet, crisp pancakes often served at festive gatherings, such as Ramadan.

BAKLAVA
A sweet and rich pastry comprising layers of phyllo (filo) pastry, honey, and nuts.

BLACK-EYED PEAS (BEANS)
Black-eyed peas are white legumes with black spots, resembling an eye. Available dried, frozen, or canned, they're a tasty and nutritious addition to salads, stews, and any vegetarian dishes.

BLACK PEPPER
Warm and intense, black peppercorns taste best when freshly ground, but pre-ground is fine for cooking.

BUCKWHEAT
Rich in soluble fiber, buckwheat is an excellent source of magnesium and calcium and contains eight essential amino acids.

BULGUR WHEAT
Bulgur is a form of cracked whole wheat that has been cleaned, parboiled, dried and ground into particles to make it easy and quick to cook.

CAROB MOLASSES
Made from the fruit of the carob pod, carob molasses has a unique fruity flavor with a hint of chocolate. It can be a chocolate substitute for people who are allergic to cocoa or dairy products.

CARAWAY
Caraway, also known as meridian fennel, comes from the fruit of a plant that's related to parsley. Warm and slightly peppery, it has a distinctive taste and works best in the very traditional Lebanese rice pudding called Meghli (page 268).

CARDAMOM
Native to the Middle East, Africa, and Scandinavia, cardamom has a compelling spicy-sweet flavor that is unlike any other spice. Although cardamoms are available as pods or ground, it's best to buy them as whole pods so the seeds can be used when needed.

CAYENNE PEPPER
Intensely fiery and pungent, cayenne peppers are long, slender, and a vibrant red when mature. Dried and ground to a powder, cayenne is popular for adding heat to a dish.

CHICKPEAS
A widely used staple in the Levantine diet, chickpeas are used in many traditional dishes, such as Classic Hummus (page 107) and Classic Falafel (page 110). Dried and canned chickpeas can be found in most supermarkets.

CHICKPEA FLOUR
Chickpea flour—also known as gram or besan flour—is naturally gluten-free and is a popular ingredient in both Middle Eastern and Indian cuisine.

RED PEPPER (CHILI) FLAKES/POWDER
A form of dried chile peppers, crushed or ground, that can be added in various amounts to soups or stews for extra heat.

CINNAMON
An aromatic and intrinsically sweet spice, cinnamon is popular in sweet pastries and desserts and adds an extra depth to savory stews.

CORIANDER (CILANTRO)

When using fresh leaves—known as cilantro—try stirring them into a dish just before serving. The ground seeds are used as a spice.

COUSCOUS (*see also* mograbieh)

Rolled semolina with a light and fluffy texture when steamed, couscous is commonly served with stews and makes a popular alternative to rice and pasta.

CUMIN

Available in seeds or ground, cumin has a strong and distinctive aroma and flavor.

DATES

At the heart of Middle Eastern cuisine and culture, there are hundreds of different species of dates, which can be enjoyed at various stages of ripeness. Completely ripe dates are most commonly eaten and their dense texture and sticky sweetness make them an excellent ingredient in cakes and sweet pastries.

FAVA (BROAD) BEANS

A staple in the Levant and Middle East, fava beans have been cultivated since ancient times. Best harvested when young and sweet, fava beans are used in soups, purees, salads and stews, such as Ful Medames (page 80).

FENNEL SEEDS

Small, oblong, and ridged, fennel seeds come in a broad range of colors, from pale yellow-brown to green. They're highly aromatic and often confused with anise, which are similar in taste and appearance. Central and Eastern European cuisines use the seeds of wild, bitter fennel, which can be compared with celery seeds.

FENUGREEK

Fenugreek, or methi, is an aromatic herb that can be added to curries, dry rubs, and even bread recipes. It is available as fresh or dried leaves or as seeds. The latter are small, brownish yellow, and mildly bitter.

FETA CHEESE

Rich and creamy, feta is a soft and brined white curd cheese traditionally made with sheep milk, or with a combination of sheep and goat milk.

FREEKEH

A staple in the Middle East, freekeh is young green wheat that is roasted and cracked. It has a pleasant nutty flavor and texture.

GINGER

Fruity and aromatic fresh ginger can be used abundantly to add an extra base note to stews. Powdered dried ginger should be used more sparingly and lends itself more favorably to sweet baked goods and pastries.

GRAPE MOLASSES

Grape molasses is a thick, sweet syrup extracted from grapes. It is a natural sweetener and was traditionally used in Lebanese villages before refined white sugar was widely available. It also has a high content of iron and is used in treating iron-related anemia.

HALLOUMI

A semi-hard, unripened, brined cheese with a high melting point so it can be broiled (grilled). Springy, mild, and tangy, fried halloumi makes a quick and tasty appetizer or snack.

HALVA

The Middle Eastern confection commonly made from ground sesame seeds and honey or sugar.

HONEY

Sticky, fragrant, and luxurious, honey makes an excellent natural sweetener and when baked, it gives a moist texture to cakes and pastries (but be careful when exposing it to heat, because it has a low burning point). It can also be drizzled over savory dishes, such as fried eggs, and used instead of sugar to sweeten your tea.

KISHK

A fine, powdery cereal made from a mixture of bulgur wheat and fermented yogurt. It can be made into soup or used as a thickener.

LABNEH

Labneh (page 95) is a type of Middle Eastern yogurt "cheese." It is made from strained lebneh (see below), which gives it a thicker consistency and richness. When strained longer, it can be rolled into balls, flavored with herbs, and stored in oil.

LEBNEH

A thick, luxurious dairy product, similar to Greek-style yogurt, lebneh is immensely popular in the Middle East as a dip or an accompaniment to both savory and sweet dishes.

LEMON LEAF

The aromatic leaves of a lemon tree are not very pleasant to eat but can be used whole in stews and soups (much like a bay leaf) to give a delicious citrus accent. They can also be wrapped around some foods, such as meatballs, cheese, or fish, before they are baked or broiled (grilled), to impart their delicate flavor.

LENTILS (GREEN/RED)
Lentils grow in pods and belong, with beans and peas, to the legume family. Low in fat and high in protein and fiber, they cook quickly, have a mild, earthy flavor, and are staples in the Middle Eastern pantry.

LIMA (BUTTER) BEANS
These large, creamy-colored beans have a soft, floury texture when cooked. Delicately flavored, lima (butter) beans are versatile and complement a wide variety of dishes.

MAHLAB
Mahlab is an aromatic spice made from the ground pits of sour cherries. It is used in the Middle East to add a sweet-sour, nutty note to breads and cookies.

MOGRABIEH (see also couscous)
Also known as Israeli, Lebanese, giant, or pearl couscous, mograbieh is a larger, slightly more doughy, version of the more familiar Moroccan couscous. Because of its size, it needs to be boiled instead of being steamed.

MUNG BEANS
These small green legumes can be eaten raw or cooked and used in both sweet and savory dishes.

NUTMEG
A gentle and earthy spice, nutmeg goes especially well with greens, such as spinach. When possible, buy whole nutmeg and grate it yourself, because it has a much more vibrant flavor than store-bought ground powder.

OKRA
This peculiar vegetable has a soft, delicate texture that melts into stews when cooked for more than a few minutes. It is a somewhat neutral vegetable that soaks up any flavors it mingles with, and it also makes for a satisfying side dish or snack when quickly sautéed whole with garlic and olive oil.

OLIVE OIL
Drizzled over hot and cold mezze, the fruity, peppery flavor of olive oil is an essential part of Middle Eastern cuisine. The purer the oil, the lower the smoking point, so be sure to use regular (instead of extra-virgin) olive oil for frying.

ORANGE FLOWER WATER
Pungently aromatic, just a drop of this concentrated floral water adds an ever-so-slightly bitter citrus note to syrups, cakes, sweet pastries, and fresh lemonade.

PEANUTS
Nuts feature prominently in Levantine dishes and peanuts, in particular, can be used in spice mixes, such as dukkah, or added for texture in stews and salads.

PEARL BARLEY
Prevalent in the Middle East, pearl barley is barley that has been processed to remove the husk and bran layers. It can be added to soups, stews, and salads, or used as a substitute for rice.

PHYLLO (FILO) PASTRY
The thin unleavened pastry dough used for making pastries such as Baklava Rolo (page 258).

PINE NUTS
Pine nuts are the edible kernels extracted from pine trees. Small and rich in flavor (especially when they're toasted), pine nuts are a staple in the Middle Eastern kitchen.

PINTO BEANS
Pinto is the Spanish word for "painted" or "spotted," which refers to the beans' appearance before they are cooked. Pinto beans are beige or cream and strewn with flecks of red. When cooked, they become tender, creamy, and pink.

PISTACHIOS
Native to the Middle East, pistachios are a member of the cashew family and happen to be one of the most nutritious of all nuts. Finely chopped pistachios are often used as a pastry filling or dessert topping.

PITA
In the Middle East, flatbreads are served with almost every meal and one of the most popular is pita bread (page 70). Wonderfully versatile, the pita can be cut in half and act as a pocket for falafel or other hot food or better yet, used to mop up sauces and stews.

POMEGRANATE
Native to Persia, the pomegranate is one of the oldest known fruits of the ancient world, and for centuries it has been revered for its flavor, color, and health benefits. Pomegranates are versatile, because they are not just popular in desserts, but they also add color, vibrancy, and sweetness to savory dishes.

POMEGRANATE MOLASSES
The sweet-sourness of pomegranates is amplified in this intense, thick syrup made from concentrated pomegranate juice. Use sparingly to add both acidity and sweetness to soups, stews, and stir-fried dishes.

PUMPKIN SEEDS
Pumpkin seeds contain concentrated sources vitamins, minerals, and amino acids. They can be roasted and eaten

whole as a snack, accent vegetable dishes, or used in sweet dishes such as the Spiced Date Oat Bars (page 229).

PUY LENTILS
Puy lentils from France are small and dark green with blue veining. They have a unique peppery flavor, retain their shape during cooking, and require less cooking time than ordinary green lentils.

QUINOA
Often referred to as a grain, quinoa is actually a seed from a vegetable related to Swiss chard, spinach, and beets (beetroot). It is not a traditional Middle Eastern grain, but I like to use it for its nutritional value (it's high in fiber and protein). It has a natural soapy coating known as saponin, a naturally occurring toxin, so it should always be rinsed thoroughly before preparation.

RICE
Whether as a supportive side dish or a hearty one-dish meal, rice plays an important role in Levantine cuisine. Rice dishes are usually made with basmati rice (I also like brown rice) and can include a range of ingredients—such as raisins, pine nuts, or meat—depending on the region.

RICE FLOUR
A type of flour made from finely milled rice, which can be used for making traditional milk and rice puddings. It is a suitable gluten-free substitute for all-purpose (plain) flour.

ROSEWATER
An intensely fragrant and evocative distillation made from steeping rose petals in water. Use sparingly to add a delicious floral note to lemonade, icings, syrups, and sweets, such as Baklava Rolo (page 258).

SEMOLINA
Semolina is a coarse grind of high-protein durum wheat kernels. Though commonly used for making pasta, semolina can also be used for making delicious traditional Lebanese cakes.

SESAME SEEDS
Touted as the "peanut" of the Middle East, sesame seeds are delicate and nutty in flavor. They are also used to make tahini, an essential Levantine ingredient.

7-SPICE SEASONING
Lebanese 7-spice (page 26) or *baharat*—not to be confused with Arabic 7-spice—is a mixture of nutmeg, ginger, allspice, fenugreek, cloves, cinnamon, and black pepper. Store in an airtight glass jar.

SHANKLISH
A Levantine cheese made from sheep or cow milk with a texture similar to feta. Salty and tangy, it can be added to salads.

SPLIT PEAS
When completely matured, dried, harvested peas split naturally into halves, making them faster to cook.

WHEAT BERRIES
Wheat berries are the entire wheat kernel—including the bran, germ, and endosperm—before it is processed. Tender, chewy, and high in fiber, they can be used like other whole grains.

STAR ANISE
A star-shape pod that contains a small seed in each of its segments. This fragrant and aromatic spice can be added to savory dishes for a subtle licorice note. Use sparingly.

SUMAC
Dark red sumac berries are usually available as a ground powder. They add a distinctive sour, citrus flavor to dishes and can be partnered with wild thyme and sesame seeds to make the spice blend Za'atar (see below and page 26).

TAHINI
Tahini (page 24) is a paste made from toasted, ground, hulled sesame seeds and is the basis for Middle Eastern dishes, such as hummus and halva. It's a staple of both Middle Eastern and Mediterranean cooking.

TURMERIC
Warm and earthy, with bitter undertones, this vibrant yellow spice is one of the key ingredients in Middle Eastern dishes. Traditionally, turmeric is used to add flavor and color to meat and vegetables in stews.

VEGETABLE BROTH (STOCK)
While it is not Middle Eastern tradition to add stock (broth) to grain dishes, I've incorporated it at times to help establish a depth of flavor in some of the recipes.

WALNUTS
In ancient Persia, walnuts were eaten only by royalty. They are a popular ingredient in sweet and savory Middle Eastern dishes and also form the basis for Muhammara (page 96), a tasty Lebanese dip.

ZA'ATAR
Za'atar is a variety of wild thyme that grows abundantly in the Middle East. It is also the name of spice blend made from the wild thyme, ground sumac, and sesame seeds. It can be used in meat and vegetable dishes.

1. Tahini 2. Lebneh 3. Lebanese 7-spice seasoning 4. Za'atar 5. Tomato paste (puree)

2 cups (9 oz/250 g)
toasted sesame seeds

1 teaspoon sea salt

½–⅔ cup (4–5 fl oz/
120–150 ml) olive oil,
depending on taste

Tahini

This really is a staple in my house, and my refrigerator is never without a jar of rich, smooth tahini. I like to use hulled seeds, and normally buy mine already toasted. Unhulled seeds work, too, but will have a slightly more bitter taste. If you can only find raw, then toast them yourself over medium heat for five minutes or so. Stir or shake the pan and watch carefully to make sure they don't burn. Depending on how powerful your processor is, the paste may not be as smooth as store-bought, but this is a small price to pay for the flavor.

Preparation time: 10 minutes
Makes: one 12-oz/350-ml jar

Put the seeds and salt into a food processor or high-speed blender with half of the oil and process. Scrape down the sides and add the rest of the oil gradually, adding more to taste, if necessary.

Pour into a sterilized jar with a screw-top lid. Store in the refrigerator for up to a month. If the mixture separates, stir to combine.

See pages 22–23 for photo

5 cups (40 fl oz/
1.2 liters) milk

⅓ cup (3 ¼ oz/90 g)
plain live bio yogurt

Lebneh

Beautifully thick homemade yogurt with a distinctive sour taste, lebneh is extremely versatile and an essential ingredient in my kitchen. It is particularly delicious with fruit, honey, and a spoonful of my compote (page 71).

Preparation time: 5 minutes + cooling and overnight standing time
Cooking time: 45 minutes
Makes: 4 cups (2 ¼ lb/1 kg)

Pour the milk into a large saucepan and bring to a boil over a very low heat, stirring occasionally. The milk should be at least 200°F/93°C and it may take up to 45 minutes.

Remove the pan from the heat and let cool until the milk is lukewarm or at 109°F/43°C. Stir in the yogurt. Cover the pan with a lid and let stand overnight, covered with a clean towel, in a warm place. It is important not to move the pan or remove the towel.

The following day, stir the yogurt once and then put it in the refrigerator for 2 days before eating.

See pages 22–23 for photo

5 tablespoons ground
allspice

3 ½ tablespoons pepper

3 ½ tablespoons ground
cinnamon

5 tablespoons ground
cloves

4 tablespoons grated
nutmeg

4 tablespoons ground
fenugreek

4 tablespoons ground
ginger

Lebanese 7-spice seasoning

**This is a classic spice-blend recipe that I have been using
for many years, but many Lebanese families have their own
version of this 7-spice blend. Just a teaspoon of it really lifts
so many dishes. For me, this seasoning captures the taste of
Lebanese food and it is a flavor that I find I miss if I don't
have it for a while, or if I am traveling abroad. It only takes
a few minutes to prepare once you have all the ingredients
together, and you can scale up the ratios to make larger
quantities, though the following recipe provides a good
amount to start out with.**

Preparation time: 5 minutes
Makes: about 1 ¾ cups (6 oz/175 g)

Mix all the ingredients together thoroughly and store in an
airtight container.

See pages 22–23 for photo

7 tablespoons fresh thyme, stems removed

2 tablespoons dried thyme

1 teaspoon dried marjoram

3 tablespoons sesame seeds, toasted

2 teaspoons sumac

sea salt to taste

3 ¼ lb/1.5 kg ripe tomatoes, roughly chopped

Za'atar

While Lebanese 7-Spice Seasoning (page 26) is another contender for the title, if there were just one flavor to sum up Lebanon, it would surely be this spice blend. Herby, fresh, and seedy, it is one ingredient I cannot live without. Once made, I keep my mix in the freezer to keep it at its best. It is versatile and I use it in many different recipes, so if you haven't used it before, I'm sure you will enjoy experimenting with it. Try it mixed with fresh grassy extra-virgin olive oil and bread before a meal.

Preparation time: 5 minutes
Cooking time: 10 minutes
Makes: 6 oz/175 g

Preheat the oven to 300°F/150°C/Gas Mark 2.

Spread the fresh thyme leaves on a baking sheet and dry in the oven for about 10 minutes, or until the leaves crumble easily. Let cool.

Crumble the thyme with your fingers. Add to the mortar with the dried thyme, marjoram, sumac, and sea salt and crush with the pestle. Once an even consistency is achieved, add the sesame seeds and stir before using.

Tomato paste

One small spoon of this transforms any dish. Just thinking about rich and savory tomato paste (puree) makes my mouth water. In Lebanon, of course, we would dry it in the sun, so it would last longer. Start with good ripened tomatoes and you will still get something delicious, even if you live somewhere cooler.

Preparation time: 15 minutes
Cooking time: 1 hour 30 minutes
Makes: ¾ cup (7 oz/200 g)

Put the tomatoes into a large saucepan, cover, and cook over medium heat for 10 minutes. Remove the lid and cook for another 1 hour 20 minutes. Remove from the heat.

Pass the tomatoes through a fine strainer (sieve) into a bowl to remove the skin and seeds.

Spoon the paste into an airtight container and store in the refrigerator. Use within a few days.

See pages 22—23 for photo

Drinks

Ⓥ Ⓖ

8 blood oranges

1 teaspoon rosewater

1 teaspoon pomegranate
molasses

2 handfuls pomegranate
seeds, to serve

Blood orange juice with pomegranate and rosewater

For this exotic and delicious drink, I have blended the juice of the distinctive blood orange with fragrant rosewater and pomegranate. Finished with the seeds of the infamous Middle Eastern pomegranate for texture, it is as pretty as it is delicious.

Preparation time: 5 minutes
Serves: 2

Juice the blood oranges, then stir the rosewater through the juice. Serve over plenty of ice with the pomegranate molasses and fresh pomegranate seeds stirred through.

Ⓥ Ⓖ

6 tablespoons grape
molasses

plenty of crushed ice

1 tablespoon golden
raisins (sultanas)

1 tablespoon pine nuts

Jallab

**Grape molasses (which is my favorite kind of molasses) is
sometimes mixed with fresh snow in Lebanon to make
a kind of sorbet. In this recipe, it makes a very popular and
traditional drink. The crushed ice makes it highly refreshing
and the golden raisins (sultanas) add fruitiness, too.**

Preparation time: 5 minutes
Serves: 2

Divide the molasses between 2 glasses, add some crushed ice,
and top with water to the desired strength.
Sprinkle on the raisins and pine nuts and serve.

ⓖ
generous 1 cup
(9 oz/250 g) honey

juice of 2 lemons

1 tablespoon rosewater

vanilla ice cream, to
serve (optional)

Rose and honey drink

Rosewater, one of the Middle East's most famous products, is an ingredient so important in our cuisine that people will travel far and wide to buy the best quality. This delicate and floral syrup can be diluted and served with ice for a refreshing drink, or drizzled over ice cream or pancakes for an easy dessert.

Preparation time: 5 minutes
Cooking time: 20 minutes
Makes: 1 ½ cups (12 fl oz/350 ml)

Put the honey into a saucepan with generous 2 cups (17 fl oz/ 500 ml) of water and stir over medium heat until all the crystals have dissolved. Bring to a boil, then remove from the heat and stir in the lemon juice and rosewater.

Return the pan to the heat and simmer, without stirring, for 10 minutes, or until the mixture thickens. Remove any foam when necessary.

Pour into sterilized bottle or jar.

Dilute with iced water to make a drink, or pour as it is over ice cream, if using.

Ⓥ Replace the honey with an equal quantity of superfine (caster) sugar.

V G

3 tea bags (black tea)

1 tablespoon honey or
superfine (caster) sugar

thinly pared zest and
juice of 2 lemons

1 tablespoon orange
flower water

plenty of ice, to serve

orange slices, to serve

Lebanese iced tea with orange flower water

This tea is wonderfully refreshing and flavorful, delicately perfumed, and sweetly lemony. Adjust the steeping time of tea to suit your tastes here, but you may also need to adjust the amount of sugar if you do so.

Preparation time: 5 minutes + steeping time and chilling time
Cooking time: 5 minutes
Serves: 6

Bring 4 ¼ cups (34 fl oz/1 liter) of water to the boil in a saucepan. Put the tea bags in and let steep for 3–5 minutes. Remove the tea bags.

Stir in the honey or sugar, lemon, and orange water. Stir until the honey or sugar is thoroughly dissolved.

Remove from the heat and let the mixture cool. Strain, chill well, and serve in glasses over plenty of ice with orange slices.

Ⓖ

zest and juice of 6 limes

zest and juice of
2 lemons

2–3 tablespoons honey

2-inch/5-cm piece fresh
ginger, peeled and sliced

20 mint leaves, plus
extra to serve

10 strawberries, hulled
and sliced

plenty of ice, to serve

lime wedges, to serve

Ginger, strawberry, and mint limeade

This twist on lemonade is flavorsome and delicious—I always enjoy its incredible aroma. The bite of fresh ginger is balanced by a hint of fresh mint. It's a perfect thirst-quencher on a hot summer's day.

Preparation time: 20 minutes + 1 ½ hours steeping time
Serves: 4–6

Put the citrus zests and juice into a heat-proof pitcher (jug). Add 2 tablespoons honey, the ginger, and mint leaves and pour in 4 ¼ cups (34 fl oz/1 liter) of boiling water. Set aside and let steep and cool completely, which will take about 1 ½ hours.
  In a blender, puree the strawberries.
  Once the steeped mixture is cold, combine with the strawberries, sweeten with more honey, if desired, then strain and serve over ice with fresh mint leaves and lime wedges.

Ⓥ Replace the honey with superfine (caster) sugar.

1. Cardamom tea 2. Mint tea 3. Black coffee 4. White coffee 5. Cinnamon-anise tea

Ⓥ Ⓖ

5 cardamom pods,
lightly crushed

1 tea bag (black tea)

3 teaspoons sugar

your choice of dairy
or plant-base milk,
warmed

Ⓖ

1 tea bag (black tea)
2 mint sprigs

honey, for drizzling

Ⓥ Ⓖ

2 teaspoons anise seeds

1 large cinnamon stick

2 lemon wedges

Cardamom tea

Preparation time: 5 minutes
Makes: 1 small pot (for 2)

Measure 2 cups (16 fl oz/475 ml) of water and bring to a boil in
a saucepan. Add the cardamom pods and bring back to a boil, then
add the tea bag and sugar. Boil for 3 minutes, strain, and serve
with warm milk of your choice.

Mint tea

**Herbal teas are a welcome break from the strong, if delicious,
Arabic coffee. I often serve them alongside falafel and other
mezze at lunchtime.**

Preparation time: 5 minutes
Makes: 1 small pot (for 2)

Put the tea bag in a teapot and pour on boiling water. Remove the
bag after 30 seconds and add the fresh mint sprigs. Steep for
5 minutes, then strain the tea and serve in heat-proof glasses with
a drizzle of honey.

Cinnamon-anise tea

Preparation time: 5 minutes
Makes: 1 small pot (for 2)

Put the spices into a small teapot and pour boiling water over
them. Steep for 3–5 minutes. Strain into heat-proof glasses and
serve each one with a lemon wedge.

See pages 40–41 for photo

4 heaping teaspoons
Lebanese (fine grind)
coffee

Black coffee

The first drink you are offered in my home, whether in South London or Lebanon, is a Lebanese coffee, generally ground with cardamom.

Rakwa is an Arabic word for a small coffeepot, usually made of copper. It has a long handle, designed to avoid burning one's hands when the pot is on the stove. The coffee is served in small espresso-like cups and saucers, presented in an almost ceremonial fashion with the rakwa on a matching circular copper tray for the family to sit round and chat together while enjoying their coffee.

If you don't have an Arabic coffeepot, simply use a small pan, preferably with a pouring lip.

Preparation time: 5 minutes
Makes: 1 small pot (rawka) for 4–6

Bring 1 ⅔ cups (14 fl oz/400 ml) water to a boil in the saucepan or rakwa. Stir in the coffee. Return to a boil, then remove from the heat and stir. Repeat this 4–5 times until the coffee no longer froths but boils smoothly. Serve immediately in espresso cups.

4 heaping teaspoons
Lebanese (fine grind)
coffee
scant 1 cup (7 fl oz/
200 ml) milk

White coffee

Preparation time: 5 minutes
Makes: 1 small pot (rawka) for 4–6

Bring 1 ⅔ cups (14 fl oz/400 ml) water to a boil in the saucepan. Stir in the coffee. Return to a boil, then remove from the heat and stir. Repeat this 4–5 times until the coffee no longer froths but boils smoothly.

Pour the milk into a small saucepan and bring just to a boil. Divide the milk between the 4 cups (you can use larger than espresso size cups with milky coffee, if preferred) and top up with the freshly brewed coffee.

See pages 40–41 for photo

Doogh

Ⓖ

1 cup (8 fl oz/250 ml) plain yogurt

1 ¼ cups (10 ½ fl oz/ 300 ml) milk

¼–½ teaspoon sea salt

2 teaspoons dried mint

plenty of ice, to serve

mint sprigs, to garnish

The sibling of India's *lassi*, this classic yogurt-base drink is wonderfully cooling in the heat.

The salt may be an acquired taste to those living in the West, but once you get used to the savory nature of the drink, it quickly becomes delicious and is a good way to replace salt lost through sweat on a hot day. If you prefer a sweeter drink, add the seeds of one vanilla bean (pod), a little honey (or sugar), and some raspberries—in addition to (or instead of) the salt.

Preparation time: 5 minutes
Serves: 2

Add the yogurt and milk to a large pitcher (jug) and stir well. Add the sea salt and dried mint and stir again. Serve over plenty of crushed ice, with fresh mint for garnish.

Ⓥ Replace the yogurt with soy yogurt and the milk with an almond, soy, or plant-base milk of your choice.

Ⓥ Ⓖ

2 bananas, peeled

2 dates, pitted

1 ¼ cups (300 ml/
10 fl oz) almond or
coconut milk (the light,
drinking kind)

2 tablespoons Tahini
(page 24)

scant ¼ cup (1 ¼ oz/
30 g) whole blanched
almonds

1 teaspoon ground
cinnamon

Date, tahini, and cinnamon smoothie

The Phoenicians, an ancient Middle Eastern people perhaps known primarily for their production of royal purple dye, were also famous for their nutritious crops, especially those of stone fruits, such as dates.

Dates were of primary importance because of their long storage life, providing food during the winter months (something that we always used to have to prepare for in Lebanon when I was a girl) and making them a useful commodity for trading farther afield. Indeed, they are still a staple in Middle Eastern cooking today.

In this recipe, I love the natural sweetness of the dates, helping to offset any bitterness present in the cinnamon. The result is a wonderful smoothie drink that has the texture of thick melted ice cream.

Preparation time: 5 minutes
Serves: 2

Put everything in a blender and puree until smooth. Serve over ice.

Ⓖ

4 heaping teaspoons
Lebanese (fine-grind)
coffee

scant 1 cup (7 fl oz/
200 ml) milk

1 tablespoon orange
flower water

Lebanese coffee with orange flower water

If you prefer a change from regular coffee and want to try a new flavor combination, this recipe using orange flower water won't disappoint. I find it's popular with friends who prefer white coffee to the more usual black coffee.

Preparation time: 5 minutes
Makes: 1 small pot (rakwa) for 4–6

Bring 1 ⅔ cups (14 fl oz/400 ml) water to a boil in the pot or saucepan. Stir in the coffee. Return to a boil, then remove from the heat and stir. Repeat this 4–5 times until the coffee no longer froths but boils smoothly.
     Pour the milk into a small saucepan and bring just to a boil. Add the orange flower water and remove from the heat. Divide the milk among 4–6 cups and top with the freshly brewed coffee.

Note: Coffee with cardamom is another flavor variation. Once the coffee boils smoothly, add 8 cardamom pods and let steep over low heat for 5 minutes. Remove the pods and serve.

Breakfast

Ⓖ

1 tablespoon coconut oil

1 cup (7 oz/200 g)
wheat berries

1 teaspoon fennel seeds

1 teaspoon ground
cinnamon

1 teaspoon ground
cardamom

3 tablespoons chopped
walnuts

3 tablespoons golden
raisins (sultanas)

sea salt

milk, to serve

Wheat berry porridge

When cooked with plenty of nuts and spices, wheat berries make a warming, comforting, and substantial breakfast, especially when lightly sweetened with raisins. Wheat berries are available raw or, occasionally, par-cooked, which reduces the cooking time. Be sure to check the cooking instructions on the package.

Preparation time: 5 minutes
Cooking time: 35 minutes
Serves: 2–4

Heat the coconut oil in a saucepan over medium heat. Add the wheat berries and the spices and cook for 5 minutes or so, stirring. Add the walnuts, a generous 2 cups (17 fl oz/500 ml) of boiling water, and a good pinch of sea salt. (The pan ingredients will sizzle when hot water is added). Return to a boil and cover, then reduce the pan, reduce the heat, and simmer for 30–40 minutes. Add more hot water if necessary. Stir occasionally to make sure the wheat berries are not sticking to the bottom of the pan. Cook until the wheat berries are tender and most of the liquid has been absorbed.

Stir in the golden raisins (sultanas) and serve warm with hot or cold milk.

Ⓥ Replace the milk with almond or soy milk.

1 cup (3 ½ oz/100 g)
organic, rolled jumbo
oats

4 cardamom pods,
lightly crushed

1 cup (8 fl oz/250 ml)
milk

2 tablespoons
pomegranate seeds

2 tablespoons raisins
(optional)

agave syrup or honey,
to drizzle

Cardamom oatmeal with fresh pomegranates

Cardamom makes an aromatic partner for creamy oatmeal in this porridge, while pomegranate seeds add pops of texture and freshness to each mouthful.

Preparation time: 2 minutes
Cooking time: 5–10 minutes
Serves: 2

Put the oats into a saucepan and add the cardamom pods. Pour in the milk and add 1 cup (8 fl oz/250 ml) water. Simmer for 10 minutes or until the oats are cooked, stirring continuously. Remove the cardamom pods.

Ladle into bowls and serve with pomegranate seeds, raisins (if using), and a drizzle of agave syrup or honey.

Ⅴ Replace the milk with soy or almond milk.

Ⓖ Use gluten-free oats.

1. Buckwheat pancakes 2. Manoushe with thyme and garlic 3. Manoushe with feta and tomato 4. Manoushe with za'atar

5. Maple, pecan, and walnut granola

1 ¼ cups (5 oz/150 g)
buckwheat flour

1 ⅔ cups (14 fl oz/
400 ml) coconut milk
beverage (the light,
drinking kind)

2 teaspoons almond
extract

3 pitted dates

pinch of pink
Himalayan salt

½ teaspoon baking
powder

juice of ½ lemon

coconut oil, for frying

Buckwheat pancakes

**These delightful pancakes are a favorite with my
grandchildren, especially when piled high with strawberries,
raspberries, and bananas. Vegan-friendly and gluten-free,
they are wonderfully light with a sweet hint of vanilla.**

Preparation time: 5 minutes
Cooking time: 5 minutes per pancake
Makes: 8 pancakes

Combine all the ingredients in a food processor, except for the
coconut oil, and blend until you have a smooth batter.

Heat the coconut oil in a skillet or frying pan on a medium
heat and add a ladleful of batter. Cook on each side for a couple
of minutes, or until golden brown, then flip to cook the other side.
Keep warm while you cook the remaining pancakes.

See pages 56–57 for photo

ⓖ

1 ½ cups
(5 oz/150 g) gluten-free
jumbo rolled oats

⅔ cup (2 oz/50 g) dried
coconut flakes

1 cup (3 ½ oz/100 g)
whole pecans

¾ cup (3 ½ oz/100 g)
chopped walnuts

⅓ cup (2 oz/50 g)
unsalted cashew nuts

3 tablespoons pumpkin
seeds

3 tablespoons sunflower
seeds

1 teaspoon ground
cinnamon

3 tablespoons coconut
oil

1 tablespoon maple
syrup

⅓ cup (2 oz/50 g) dried
apricots, chopped

⅓ cup (2 oz/50 g) dried
cranberries

milk, Lebneh (page 25),
and fresh fruit, to serve

Maple, pecan, and walnut granola

A gently spiced breakfast, delicious served with seasonal fresh fruit and lebneh or milk.

Preparation time: 5 minutes
Cooking time: 25–30 minutes
Serves: 6–8

Preheat the oven to 275°F/140°C/Gas Mark 1 and line a baking sheet with parchment (baking) paper.

Combine all the ingredients except the dried fruit in a bowl and mix together well. Spread out evenly on the prepared baking sheet and bake for 20–30 minutes, or until golden. Turn the mixture around halfway through cooking.

Remove from the oven and let cool, then mix through the dried fruit.

Serve with your favorite fresh fruit, yogurt, and milk.

Ⓥ Serve with soy yogurt and plant-base milk.

See pages 56–57 for photo

V

2 cups (9 oz/250 g) whole wheat (strong wholemeal) bread flour

2 cups (8 oz/250 g) all-purpose (plain) flour, plus extra for dusting

2 ½ teaspoons active dry (fast-action)

1 teaspoon salt

2 tablespoons olive oil, plus extra for greasing

Manoushe

We often say, "The house is empty if the breadbasket is not full." These incredible breads are one of Lebanon's favorite street snacks and are regularly eaten for breakfast. Chewy and crisp, with an array of topping choices, they are hard to resist.

Preparation time: 20 minutes + 2 ½ hours rising time
Cooking time: 7-10 minutes
Makes: 8 flatbreads

In a large mixing bowl, combine the flours, yeast, and salt. Slowly add 1 cup (8 fl oz/250 ml) lukewarm water, mixing with a wooden spoon until a dough forms. You may need to add a little more water to bring the dough together.

Knead for a few minutes on an oiled work surface until the dough starts to become a little more elastic. Put the dough into a lightly oiled bowl, cover with a dish cloth, and let rise in a warm place for about 2 hours, or until doubled in size.

Knead again and divide into 4 even portions. Put each piece of dough into a separate oiled bowl and let rise again for 30 minutes.

Preheat the oven to 350°F/180°C/Gas Mark 4.

Divide each ball in half and roll out into circles about 4 ½– 5 ½ inches/12–14 cm in diameter and ¼ inch/½ cm thick.

Add the topping of your choice (page 61), then bake the flatbreads on baking sheets for 10 minutes, or until bubbling and golden brown. Serve warm.

Ⓖ Replace the flour with 3 ⅓ cups (1 lb/500 g) gluten-free bread flour blend and combine with yeast, sugar, and salt. Mix 1 cup (8 fl oz/250 ml) warm water with 2 tablespoons olive oil, 1 egg, and 1 teaspoon white wine vinegar. Whisk together well, then pour slowly into the flour, mixing with a wooden spoon until a dough forms. Knead to a smooth dough and let rise for 1 hour. Divide into 4 pieces and let each rise for another 30 minutes. Divide each in half again and roll into circles 6 inches/15 cm in diameter. Add toppings and bake, as above.

See pages 56–57 for photo

Ⓥ Ⓖ

1 tablespoon thyme
leaves

1 teaspoon Lebanese
7-Spice Seasoning
(page 26)

2 garlic cloves, crushed

4 tablespoons olive oil

Thyme and garlic

Mix the ingredients together to make a paste and brush onto each
flatbread before baking.

Ⓖ

5 oz/150 g feta cheese,
crumbled

8 cherry tomatoes,
quartered

olive oil

2 tablespoons chopped
mint

Feta and tomato

Top each flatbread with some feta and tomatoes and drizzle
on a little oil. Sprinkle on the mint once the flatbreads are out
of the oven.

Ⓥ Ⓖ

¾ cup (3 oz/80 g)
Za'atar (page 27)

4 tablespoons olive oil

Olive oil and za'atar

Mix the spices and oil together well, and brush onto each
flatbread before baking.

See pages 56–57 for photo

11 ¼ oz/320 g ready-rolled puff pastry

4 tablespoons olive oil

3 tablespoons Za'atar (page 27)

⅓ cup (3 ½ oz/100g) Lebneh (page 25)

salt and pepper

Za'atar and lebneh breakfast pastries

Za'atar, a quintessential flavors of the Middle East, pairs wonderfully with the creaminess of lebneh and crisp, flaky pastry for an indulgent breakfast. It's even better if you can make your own za'atar.

Preparation time: 15 minutes
Cooking time: 20 minutes
Makes: 12

Preheat the oven to 400°F/200°C/Gas Mark 6 and line a baking sheet with parchment (baking) paper.

Unroll the pastry and place onto a lightly floured work surface. Spread the lebneh over the pastry as evenly as possible, leaving a 1 ¼-inch/3-cm edge.

Mix the olive oil and za'atar together and drizzle it over the pastry. Season with salt and pepper.

Carefully roll the pastry up as tightly as possible. Put the rolled pastry into the freezer for 5 minutes. Remove and, using a serrated knife, cut the roll into 12 even slices. Place each slice on the baking sheet, spacing them generously, and bake in the oven for 15 minutes, until golden.

Rosewater pancakes with pistachio and honey

1 ¼ cup (5 oz/ 140 g) all-purpose (plain) flour

pinch of salt

scant 1 cup (7 fl oz/ 200 ml) milk

2 eggs

1 teaspoon rosewater

olive oil, for greasing

honey or maple syrup, to drizzle

1 cup (5 oz/150 g) pistachios, finely chopped

Known as *ataif*, this is usually a crispy and indulgent Arabic treat. Here, I make a breakfast-friendly version that is much less sweet, but still has that fragrant yet subtle flavor of rosewater contrasted with the classic combination of crunchy pistachios and sweet honey. An 8-inch/20-cm crepe pan is perfect for this recipe.

Preparation time: 10 minutes
Cooking time: 5 minutes per pancake
Serves: 4 (1 lb/450 g batter makes eight 8-inch/20-cm pancakes)

Put the flour and salt into a bowl. Make a well in the center, add the eggs (or add the egg substitute), then pour in the milk slowly.

Add the rosewater and whisk the mixture thoroughly to make a smooth, pourable batter.

Grease the crepe pan with oil. Set over medium heat and add enough batter to cover the bottom of the pan. Cook for 2–3 minutes, or until the edges of the pancake begin to pull away from the pan. Flip the pancake over and cook the other side for another 2–3 minutes. Transfer to a warm plate while you cook the remaining pancakes.

Serve the pancakes immediately with drizzled honey and pistachios.

Ⓥ Replace the milk with soy or almond milk, then replace the eggs with 2 teaspoons egg substitute (such as Orgran No Egg) and add an additional ⅔ cup (5 fl oz/150 ml) water.

Ⓖ Substitute the flour with a gluten-free flour and add an additional 4 tablespoons water or milk.

2 potatoes, cut into
½-inch/1-cm cubes

1 tablespoon olive oil

1 onion, chopped

2 garlic cloves, crushed

salt and pepper

2 tomatoes, chopped

4 eggs

chopped parsley leaves,
to serve

Breakfast eggs with tomatoes

**This recipe, known at *mashlouka*, is a regular choice in
our house. The scrambled eggs make for a satisfying and
wholesome breakfast.**

Preparation time: 10 minutes
Cooking time: 20 minutes
Serves: 2

Parboil the potatoes in boiling water for 5 minutes or until just
cooked. Drain well.

Heat a skillet or frying pan until hot, then add the olive oil and
onion. Sauté for a few minutes or until lightly golden. Add the
garlic and cook for 1 minute.

Add the potato cubes to the pan and cook on medium heat
until the potato is cooked and golden on all sides. Season well with
salt and pepper, then add the chopped tomatoes and cook for a
few more minutes.

Lightly whisk the eggs together in a bowl, and pour over the
potato mixture. Cook over medium heat, mixing the eggs around
in the pan to scramble.

Sprinkle with parsley and serve immediately.

Ⓥ Replace the eggs with 7 oz/200 g silken tofu. Drain and pat the
tofu dry and scramble it in a bowl. Add it to the potato mixture,
then sprinkle on the cumin. Cook over medium heat, stirring
to be sure of even cooking, until browned. Sprinkle with
parsley and serve immediately.

1. Pita bread 2. Rose plum jam 3. Arabic flatbread 4. Strawberry, raspberry, and honey compote 5. Almond bread

6. Apricot almond conserve

Pita bread

2 ½ teaspoons active dry (fast-action) yeast

1 tablespoon honey or superfine (caster) sugar

3 cups (1 lb/450 g) white bread (strong white) flour, plus extra for dusting

1 ½ teaspoons sea salt

½ cup (3 ½ fl oz/100 ml) warm milk

vegetable oil, for greasing

Probably the most famous bread to come from the Middle East, pita is wholesome and versatile. I like to fill the pocket with falafel or hummus and salad, but it is good with anything savory. Making pita at home can be so much better than what you can buy in supermarkets, and there is something really satisfying about baking fresh bread.

Preparation time: 25 minutes + 1 hour rising time
Cooking time: 10 minutes
Makes: 6

Measure out ⅔ cup (5 fl oz/150 ml) lukewarm water. Spoon 3 tablespoons into a small bowl and stir in the yeast to dissolve. Stir in the honey or sugar.

Sift together the flour and salt into a large mixing bowl and stir in the yeast mixture. Gradually add the remaining water and milk, mixing with a wooden spoon until a dough forms.

Turn out onto a floured work surface and knead for about 10 minutes, until smooth and elastic.

Shape the dough into a ball, then put it into a bowl, cover with oiled plastic wrap (clingfilm), and let rise for 1 hour, or until roughly doubled in size.

Preheat the oven to 450°F/230°C/Gas Mark 8.

Divide the dough into 6 equal pieces and roll each one out on a floured work surface to an 8-inch/20-cm circle. Lift onto baking sheets and bake for 7–9 minutes, or until risen and golden. These pitas are best served warm.

Ⓥ Replace the milk with almond milk.

See pages 68–69 for photo

Ⓥ Ⓖ

8 firm plums, halved
and pitted

juice of ½ lemon

1 ¼ cups (9 oz/250 g)
granulated sugar

1 tablespoon rosewater

Rose plum jam

Fragrant rosewater and juicy plums come together here for a mouth-watering and pretty colored jam. As anyone who knows Lebanese food will be aware, jams have a very important place in our pantry. This is partly because we like them so much, but the real reason is that making jam is simply an incredibly useful way to preserve and make the most of our fruit. Having jars of different jams in the cupboard during the winter months is a must.

Preparation time: 15 minutes
Cooking time: 1 hour 15 minutes
Makes: one 1-lb/450-g jar

Place the fruit, lemon juice, and 4 tablespoons water into a heavy saucepan and bring to a boil, stirring frequently. Reduce the heat, cover, and simmer for about 40 minutes until the plums have softened. Stir occasionally with a wooden spoon.

Keep over low heat and add the sugar and rosewater. Stir continuously until the sugar has dissolved. Turn up the heat and stir continuously until the mixture comes to a rapid boil.

Continue stirring over high heat until the jam reaches setting point on a candy (sugar) thermometer. If you don't have a thermometer, the jam is ready when the mixture starts to stick or set on the sides of the pan or starts to set when you drop it from your wooden spoon.

Remove the pan from the heat. Spoon the jam into a 16-fl oz/450-g sterilized jar, leaving a ½-inch/1-cm head space. Let cool, then cover, seal, and label. Store in a cool cupboard for up to 6 months and refrigerate once opened.

See pages 68–69 for photo

2 cups (11 oz/300 g)
strong white bread flour,
plus extra for dusting

⅔ cup (3 ½ oz/100 g)
strong whole wheat
(wholemeal) flour

2 ½ teaspoons active
dry (fast-action) yeast

½ teaspoon salt

4 ½ tablespoons (2 ½ oz/
65 g) butter, melted, plus
extra for greasing

Arabic flatbread

**I serve Arabic flatbread (also known as *khoubz*) with nearly
every meal, whether it is to mop-up stews or soups, wrap
around falafel or salad or spread with Lebneh (page 25) and
Za'atar (page 27) for a moreish snack.**

Preparation time: 20 minutes + 1 hour rising time
Cooking time: 10 minutes
Makes: 10

Sift both flours into a bowl and add the yeast and salt. Make a
well in the middle of the flour and pour in the melted butter.
Gradually mix in a scant 1 cup (7 fl oz/200 ml) of lukewarm water
to form a dough.

Turn out onto a floured work surface and knead for a few
minutes until smooth.

Put the dough in a lightly greased bowl, cover with a dish
cloth and leave in a warm place for 1 hour, or until doubled
in size.

Preheat the oven to 425°F/220°C/Gas Mark 7 and lightly
grease 3 baking sheets with butter.

Divide the dough into 10 equal pieces and roll each one out
on a floured work surface to a thin circle. Lift onto the prepared
baking sheets and bake for 8–10 minutes, or until risen and just
starting to brown.

See pages 68–69 for photo

scant ½ cup (3 ½ fl oz/
100 ml) honey

1 tablespoon
pomegranate molasses

1 ¾ cups (10 oz/275 g)
strawberries, halved
and hulled

2 cups (10 oz/275 g)
raspberries

Strawberry, raspberry, and honey compote

A wonderful summer compote, which I like to serve alongside yogurt and fresh fruit or on top of one of my sorbets. Along with the honey and the natural sugars of the fruit, it is the pomegranate molasses that brings the rich, complex sweetness to this compote. The raspberry adds just a slight sharpness to contrast with the smooth and sweet flavors.

Preparation time: 5 minutes
Cooking time: 5–10 minutes
Serves: 4

Pour the honey into a saucepan, add ½ cup (4 fl oz/120 ml) of water, and heat gently to dissolve the honey. Bring to simmering point, then add the pomegranate molasses and berries, stir well, and remove from the heat.

Let the compote cool, then refrigerate and eat within 3–4 days.

See pages 68–69 for photo

1 ⅔ cups (8 oz/220 g)
white bread (strong
white) flour, plus extra
for dusting

1 ½ cups (8 oz/220 g)
strong brown bread
(strong wholemeal) flour

1 ¼ cups (4 oz/120 g)
almond meal (ground
almonds)

1 teaspoon sea salt

2 ½ teaspoons active
dry (fast-action) yeast

1 tablespoon olive oil,
plus extra for greasing

Almond bread

**Adding almond meal (ground almonds) to this loaf lends
a subtle sweetness and makes the bread particularly good for
toasting. It's a nice way to add some variety to the bread
basket. I love it covered in homemade jam!**

Preparation time: 15 minutes + 1–2 hours rising time
Cooking time: 45–50 minutes
Makes: 2 × 1 lb/450 g loaves

Measure out 1 ¼ cups (10 fl oz/300 ml) lukewarm water.

Put the flours, almond meal (ground almonds), and salt in
a mixing bowl. Make a well in the middle and add the yeast and
olive oil, with a little of the warm water. Gradually work in the
remaining warm water using a wooden spoon or your hands,
until fully incorporated.

Turn out onto a floured work surface and knead for around
5 minutes until smooth and elastic.

Brush two 4 × 8-inch (10 × 20-cm) loaf pans with olive oil.

Divide the dough in half and place in the prepared pans. Cover
with a damp dish cloth and let rise in a warm place for 1–2 hours,
or until nearly doubled in size.

Preheat the oven to 400°F/200°C/Gas Mark 6.

Bake the bread for 40–45 minutes, or until it sounds hollow
when the bottom is tapped. Remove the loaves from the pans
and transfer to a wire rack to cool.

See pages 68–69 for photo

Ⓥ Ⓖ

2 cups (9 oz/250 g)
dried apricot halves

½ cup (3 ½ oz/100 g)
granulated sugar

scant 1 cup (3 oz/80 g)
flaked almonds

Apricot almond conserve

Slivered (flaked) almonds and sweet apricots make a scrumptious jam that is delicious spread thickly on a toasted slice of my Almond Bread (page 74). There is simply nothing better for a special breakfast, or when whiling away a sunny fall (autumn) afternoon.

Preparation time: 10 minutes + overnight soaking time
Cooking time: 1 hour
Makes: one 15-fl oz/450-g) jar

Put the apricots into a bowl and cover with cold water. Let soak overnight.

The next day, drain off any excess water from the apricots.

Pour 1 cup (8 fl oz/250 ml) of water into a heavy saucepan, add the sugar, and heat gently until the sugar dissolves. Add the drained apricots.

Bring to a boil, then reduce the heat, cover, and simmer for 20 minutes, stirring occasionally with a wooden spoon. Add the almonds and continue to cook for another 30 minutes, stirring occasionally.

Remove the pan from the heat. Spoon the conserve into a 15-fl oz/450-g sterilized jar, leaving a ½-inch/1-cm head space. Let cool, then cover, seal, and label. Store in a cool cupboard for up to 6 months and refrigerate once opened.

See pages 68–69 for photo

1 teaspoon olive oil

½ onion, finely chopped

2 Lebanese white
or regular zucchini
(courgettes)

2 eggs

2–3 tablespoons
chopped parsley

1–2 tablespoons
chopped mint

sea salt and pepper

Lebanese omelet

This light but sustaining breakfast is classic Lebanese fare (known as a zucchini *iijeh*) and can be eaten by itself or tucked inside a Pita Bread (page 70) with sliced tomatoes. I particularly enjoy it in the winter when I'm in the mood for something warming.

Lebanese white zucchini (courgettes) are shorter and more bulbous than the ordinary variety, and either can be used in this recipe.

Preparation time: 5 minutes
Cooking time: 10 minutes
Serves: 1

Heat the oil in a 6-inch/15-cm skillet or frying pan. Add the onion and a little sea salt and cook until slightly caramelized.

Slice the zucchini (courgette) in half lengthwise and use a teaspoon to scoop out the flesh. Coarsely chop the flesh and add to the onions in the pan.

Whisk the eggs in a bowl with the herbs and salt and pepper. Add to the skillet and cook over a low–medium heat.

Once the omelet has set around the edges of the pan, carefully flip it over and cook the other side for another minute. Transfer to a plate and serve immediately.

Ⓥ Replace the eggs with 11 oz/300 g silken tofu and 2 tablespoons hummus. Combine in a food processor and blend together with enough water to make an egglike batter. Once added to the skillet, cook over a low–medium heat. Once it has set around the edges of the pan, finish the omelet off under a hot broiler (grill) for 2 minutes, which will be easier than flipping it.

1 cup (7 oz/200 g) pearl barley, rinsed

1 teaspoon ground cinnamon

⅔ cup (3 oz/80 g) chopped walnuts, toasted

2 tablespoons superfine (caster) sugar

¼ cup (1 ½ oz/40 g) pomegranate seeds

Harisa

Harisa (not to be mistaken with harissa, the Tunisian hot chili paste) is a celebratory barley dish prepared in villages across Lebanon, where it is often cooked on days of religious significance in a huge cauldron at a village gathering.

Villagers each bring ingredients to add to the pot the night before a saint's day. When the sun rises, it is eaten in the churchyard. In my village, you eat it on the 7th of August (St. Dominic's Day). In some parts of the country, it is eaten on New Year's Day to bring good luck for the coming year.

It is traditionally made with meat, but my vegetarian version is lighter and fresher. My father-in-law used to eat harisa made to my recipe every morning, without fail, because he believed it to be a health food.

Preparation time: 5 minutes + overnight soaking time
Cooking time: 1 hour
Serves: 4

Soak the barley in cold water overnight.

Drain and rinse the barley, then put it into a large saucepan with the cinnamon and 2 ½ cups (20 fl oz/600 ml) water and bring to a boil.

Lower the heat and simmer the barley for 1–1 ½ hours, or until tender, but still with a little bite. Top with more boiling water as necessary (it evaporates quickly), stirring occasionally to prevent it from sticking to the bottom of the pan. Be careful not to add too much water, because it can become stodgy.

Stir in the walnuts, sugar, and pomegranate and serve warm.

2 (14-oz/400-g) cans ful
medames

2 garlic cloves, minced

2 teaspoons ground
cumin

1 small bunch fresh
parsley, leaves chopped,
plus extra to garnish

juice of 1 lemon

olive oil, to drizzle

sea salt and pepper

Arabic Flatbread
(page 72), to serve

Ful medames

**A quintessential Middle Eastern dish, ful medames is a
cumin-spiced stew that is often eaten for breakfast (it's Heni's
favorite), but is also wonderful as part of a mezze. The
special canned, cooked fava (broad) beans are available in
Middle Eastern stores and large supermarkets and are worth
hunting out.**

Preparation time: 5 minutes
Cooking time: 5–10 minutes
Serves: 4

Drain away half the liquid from the can of ful medames. Transfer
to a saucepan over medium heat and bring to a boil. Cook for
5–10 minutes, then remove from the heat and stir in the garlic,
cumin, parsley (reserve a little extra for garnish), and lemon juice.
Drizzle with olive oil, season generously, and sprinkle
with coarsely chopped parsley. Serve with plenty of flatbread.

Dips and Mezzes

1–2 tablespoons olive oil

4 teaspoons Za'atar
(page 27)

1 teaspoon salt, plus
extra to taste

⅔ cup (3 ½ oz/100 g)
cashew nuts

⅔ cup (3 ½ oz/100 g)
whole almonds, skin on
or off

Za'atar-spiced nuts

These delicious nuts are the perfect way to whet your appetite for a mezze spread. They are herby, salty, and seedy to just the right degree.

Preparation time: 5 minutes
Cooking time: 10–15 minutes
Serves: 4

Preheat the oven to 350°F/180°C/Gas Mark 4.

Put the oil, za'atar, and salt into a large bowl and mix to form a paste. Add the casher nuts and almonds and stir until they are coated evenly.

Sprinkle the coated nuts out on a baking sheet and roast for 8 minutes. Take them out of the oven, shake well, and return to the oven for another 5 minutes.

Pour the roasted nuts onto some paper towels to absorb excess oil. Let cool and season to taste.

Ⓥ Ⓖ

1 ¾ lb/800 g fresh
or frozen fava (broad)
beans

3 ½ oz/100 g
chargrilled artichoke
hearts (from a jar or
delicatessen)

1 garlic clove

1 teaspoon ground
cumin

juice of ½ lemon

salt and pepper

TO SERVE

olive oil, to drizzle

lemon wedges (optional)

Fava bean and artichoke dip

Fava (broad) beans make a refreshing dip. I find that pairing them with artichokes, lemon, and spices provides a tasty twist and is perfect for dunking your falafel or flatbread into.

Preparation time: 15 minutes
Cooking time: 3–4 minutes
Serves: 4

Put the fava (broad) beans into a saucepan and cover with boiling water. Return to a simmer, cover, and cook for 2–4 minutes, or until tender.

Plunge the beans into cold water, then pop them out of their gray outer skins.

Put all the ingredients into a food processor, season with salt and pepper, and process until the desired consistency is achieved. Drizzle generously with olive oil and serve with lemon wedges, if using.

3 eggplants (aubergines)

2 small cloves garlic

2 tablespoons Tahini
(page 24)

juice of ½ lemon

1 tablespoon olive oil

handful pomegranate
seeds, for sprinkling

salt and pepper

Baba ganoush

Creamy, garlicky, and addictive, it is no wonder that baba ganoush is famous around the globe. For the perfect accompaniment, carefully toast some Pita Bread (page 70) directly over a low gas flame of your stove and use to dip them in.

Preparation time: 10 minutes + cooling time
Cooking time: 30–45 minutes
Serves: 4–6

Preheat the oven to 400°F/200°C/Gas Mark 6. Put the eggplants (aubergines) onto a baking sheet, prick them all over with a fork, then roast in the oven for 30–45 minutes, until soft. Once cool enough to handle, peel the skin off and discard. Set the flesh aside to cool completely.

Put the garlic into a mortar with a little salt and crush with a pestle, then add the tahini and lemon juice and mix well.

When the eggplant flesh is cool, chop it finely, transfer to a bowl, and add the garlic-tahini mixture. Season well and thoroughly combine all the ingredients. Place on a serving plate, then drizzle with olive oil and sprinkle on the pomegranate seeds.

1. Nan's kibbeh 2. Butternut hummus 3. Almond hummus 4. Sesame-crusted parsley falafel 5. Labneh 6. Chili chickpea crackers

2 (11 oz/300 g) sweet potatoes

generous 1 cup
(7 oz/200 g) quinoa

1 onion, grated

1 teaspoon ground cumin

1 teaspoon Lebanese 7-Spice Seasoning (page 26)

1 teaspoon ground coriander

1 teaspoon sumac

½ teaspoon cayenne pepper

½ teaspoon ground nutmeg

½ bunch parsley, leaves finely chopped

juice of 1 lemon

salt and pepper

sunflower oil, for greasing

Nan's kibbeh

This spicy, sweet kibbeh is a version of a recipe that dates back generations in my family and is still a firm favorite. We have it almost every weekend in our home. I have combined sweet potato with quinoa (rather than traditional bulgur wheat) so anyone with gluten intolerances can also enjoy it.

Preparation time: 15 minutes
Cooking time: 1 hour and 45 minutes
Serves: 8–10

Preheat the oven to 400°F/200°C/Gas Mark 6.

Bake the sweet potatoes for 45–60 minutes, or until tender. Remove from the oven, slice them open, and let steam-dry for 15 minutes.

Meanwhile, cook the quinoa as instructed on the package. Drain, rinse, and squeeze out any excess water, then set aside.

When the sweet potatoes are cool enough to handle, scoop out the flesh, put it into a bowl, and mash with a fork. Add the quinoa, the onion, spices, parsley, and lemon juice and season with salt and pepper. Mix well until thoroughly combined.

Grease a 12-inch/30-cm springform cake pan with a little oil. Press the mixture into the prepared pan. Score the surface into 8 portions and score each portion in a crisscross pattern. Use the end of a wooden spoon or your finger to make a ¾-inch/2-cm hole in the center. Bake for 1 hour, then remove from the oven and let cool before cutting.

See pages 90–91 for photo

ⓋⒼ

14 oz/400 g butternut
squash, peeled and cut
into chunks

2 garlic cloves, roughly
chopped

1 (14-oz/400-g) can
chickpeas, drained

4 tablespoons Tahini
(page 24)

2 teaspoons sea salt

juice of 2 lemons

2 tablespoons extra-
virgin olive oil, plus
extra to serve

chopped parsley leaves,
to serve (optional)

ⓋⒼ

2 (14-oz/400-g) cans
chickpeas

2 garlic cloves, roughly
chopped

4 tablespoons Tahini
(page 24)

juice of 2 lemons

2 teaspoons sea salt

2 tablespoons extra-
virgin olive oil

1 cup (3 ½ oz/100 g)
almond meal (ground
almonds)

handful slivered (flaked)
almonds (optional)

Butternut hummus

**Butternut squash brings an extra creaminess to traditional
hummus and adds a lovely brightness and sweetness too.**

Cooking time: 10 minutes
Preparation time: 10 minutes
Serves: 6

Steam the squash for 10 minutes, or until tender.

Put into a food processor with all the other ingredients, except
for the parsley, and process until smooth. Add extra lemon juice
and olive oil according to taste.

Transfer into a dish and serve with a sprinkling of parsley, if
using, and a generous drizzle of olive oil.

Almond hummus

**For many years, I have been a purist when it comes to
hummus. Why change something that is already so delicious?
But I did wonder what it would be like to add some different
ingredients for a change, and the answer is, brilliant! I still
usually serve the classic one, too, but it is lovely to experiment
with different flavors and textures.**

Preparation time: 5 minutes
Serves: 6

Drain the chickpeas, reserving scant ½ cup (3 ½ fl oz/100 ml)
of liquid from the can.

Put the chickpeas and liquid into a food processor with all the
other ingredients, except for the slivered (flaked) almonds,
and process until smooth. Add extra lemon juice and olive oil
according to taste.

Transfer the hummus to a bowl and serve with a good drizzle
of olive oil and the slivered almonds, if using.

See pages 90–91 for photo

¾ cup (7 oz/200 g)
dried chickpeas

½ teaspoon baking soda
(bicarbonate of soda)

3 garlic cloves, coarsely
chopped

1 small onion, chopped

⅓ cup (¾ oz/20 g)
chopped parsley

1 teaspoon ground
cumin

½ teaspoon pepper

1 teaspoon salt

1 teaspoon dried mint

1 ½ teaspoons ground
coriander

⅓ cup (2 ½ oz/50 g)
sesame seeds

sunflower oil, for frying

Sesame-crusted parsley falafel

I always think that the sesame seeds on the outside of these falafel make them so pretty, and the flavor combines wonderfully with the parsley.

Preparation time: 30 minutes + overnight soaking
and chilling time
Cooking time: 30 minutes
Makes: 20 falafel

Soak the chickpeas overnight with the baking soda (bicarbonate of soda).

Drain the chickpeas well and discard any skins, then put them into a food processor with all the other ingredients, except for the sesame seeds and oil, and process until smooth. Transfer the mixture to a dish and press down with the back of a spoon. Cover and place in the refrigerator for a few hours to chill.

Using a falafel scoop, make 20 falafel, rinsing out the scoop each time with hot water. If you don't have a scoop, take walnut-size pieces of the mixture and shape them into small oval patties with damp hands. Roll each falafel in sesame seeds to coat.

Pour sunflower oil into a saucepan to depth of 4 inches/10 cm. Heat the oil to 350°F/180°C, or until a cube of bread browns in 30 seconds. Carefully fry the falafel in batches for 1–2 minutes, until golden. Make sure the oil is back up to temperature between batches. Remove with a slotted spoon and drain on paper towels. Serve hot.

See pages 90–91 for photo

Ⓖ

1 quantity Lebneh
(page 25)

salt

extra-virgin olive oil,
for drizzling

paprika, for dusting

Ⓥ

2 ¼ cups (9 oz/250 g)
chickpea (gram) flour,
plus extra for dusting

1 teaspoon baking
powder

½ cup (2 ½ oz/75 g)
toasted sesame seeds

1 teaspoon chili powder,
or more to taste

1 teaspoon fine sea salt

3 tablespoons olive oil,
plus extra for brushing

Labneh

This strained yogurt is wonderfully thick and indulgent. It makes a great dip for mezze, and is also a perfect sandwich filling, if you're in a hurry. Spread it on toast and sprinkle with za'atar for a delicious snack, too. Make your own Lebneh for this recipe, or use good-quality yogurt.

Preparation time: 5 minutes
Serves: 4–6

Line a strainer (sieve) with a double thickness of cheesecloth (muslin) and set over a large bowl. Pour in the lebneh, cover, and set aside at room temperature for about 3 hours until all the liquid has drained off.

Check occasionally to make sure the bottom of the strainer is not touching the liquid and drain off if it is.

Season the lebneh with salt to taste, then spread out on a plate. Drizzle with olive oil and dust with paprika. Best chilled before serving.

Chili chickpea crackers

These savory crackers are ideal to serve alongside soups or stews for a more substantial meal. Chickpea (gram) flour is really flavorful when baked, and is enhanced further by a little warmth from the spices.

Preparation time: 10 minutes
Cooking time: 20 minutes
Makes: 8

Preheat the oven to 350°F/180°C/Gas Mark 4 and line 2 baking sheets with parchment (baking) paper.

Place all the dry ingredients in a mixing bowl and stir to combine. Stir in the olive oil then gradually add 6–8 tablespoons cold water, a trickle at a time. Stir well, bringing the mixture together to form a smooth dough.

Turn the dough out on a floured work surface. Roll to a thickness of ¾ inch/1 cm, and use a pastry cutter to stamp out 8 × 3 ¼-inch/8-cm circles. Brush the tops with olive oil.

Bake for 15 minutes, or until golden brown. Remove from the oven and cool on a wire rack.

Ⓖ For a gluten-free option, replace the baking powder with a gluten-free option such as Fleischman's or Magic.

See pages 90–91 for photo

3 red bell peppers, seeded
and cut into strips

olive oil, to drizzle

½ Arabic Flatbread
(page 72)

½ teaspoon cayenne
pepper

½ teaspoon smoked
chili powder

1 ¼ cups (5 oz/150 g)
chopped walnuts

1 tablespoon
pomegranate molasses

juice of ½ lemon

1 tablespoon plain
(natural) yogurt

1 tablespoon chopped
parsley

2 tablespoons pine nuts,
soaked in water for
20 minutes, then drained

salt and pepper

Pita Bread (page 70),
to serve

Muhammara

A lesser-known sibling of baba ganoush and hummus, but still making a regular appearance on our table, this walnut-bell pepper dip is a winning combination of red bell pepper, smoked spices, sweet molasses, and bread crumbs.

Preparation time: 10 minutes
Cooking time: 30 minutes
Serves: 4–6

Preheat the oven to 400°F/200°C/Gas Mark 6.

Place the strips of bell pepper on a baking sheet and drizzle lightly with olive oil. Roast the bell peppers for about 30 minutes, until soft. Remove from the oven, put into a bowl, and cover with plastic wrap (clingfilm).

Put the flatbread onto a clean baking sheet and bake for 5 minutes until golden and crisp. Transfer to a food processor and process to fine bread crumbs. Transfer the bread crumbs to a bowl and mix with the cayenne pepper. Season well. Set aside 1 tablespoon of bread crumbs for garnish.

Pour a scant ½ cup (3 ½ fl oz/100 ml) water into the food processor and add the roasted peppers, chili powder, walnuts, pomegranate molasses, and lemon juice. Add the spiced bread crumbs and pulse until the mixture is fine.

Transfer the muhammara to a bowl. Season with salt and pepper, stir in the yogurt, and sprinkle with chopped parsley, and pine nuts. Top with the reserved bread crumbs and serve with pita bread.

Ⓥ Replace the yogurt with soy yogurt.

Ⓖ For a gluten-free option, replace the bread crumbs with crumbs from gluten-free bread.

Ⓖ

2 ripe avocados

½ cup (2 ½ oz/75 g) fresh or frozen peas

2 tablespoons Tahini (page 24)

juice of 1 lemon

1 garlic clove

1 teaspoon honey (optional)

½ teaspoon cumin seeds, toasted

salt and pepper

1 small bunch mint leaves, plus extra to garnish

handful pine nuts, toasted

Pita Bread (page 70), toasted, to serve

Avocado tahini dip

This Middle Eastern take on guacamole is extra-delicious with the addition of pine nuts and tahini.

Preparation time: 5 minutes
Cooking time: 2–3 minutes
Serves: 4

Cook the peas in boiling water for 2–3 minutes (less if they are fresh), and refresh immediately in cold water to retain color.

Combine all the ingredients, except the pine nuts, in a food processor and process until smooth.

Finish with the pine nuts and garnish with a sprig of mint. Serve with toasted pita bread.

Ⓥ Replace the honey with agave syrup.

Ⓖ

1 small bunch fresh
mint, leaves chopped

1 small bunch fresh
parsley, leaves chopped

1 garlic clove, finely
chopped

4 tablespoons olive oil

1 teaspoon sumac

3 ½ oz/250 g halloumi,
sliced into 8 pieces

lemon wedges, to serve

Halloumi with sumac and mint

Crisp, golden, salty halloumi—paired with tangy sumac and refreshing mint—is the star of the show in any mezze.

Preparation time: 10 minutes + marinating time
Cooking time: 6–8 minutes
Serves: 2–4

Mix together the mint, parsley, garlic, olive oil, and sumac. Arrange the halloumi slices in a shallow ovenproof dish and pour the dressing over them, turning so each slice is covered. Let marinate for 10 minutes.
    Preheat the broiler (grill) on a high setting.
    Put the dish under the broiler and broil (grill) the halloumi for 4 minutes on each side, or until golden and the edges become crisp. Remove from the heat and serve warm with lemon wedges.

2 ½ cups (15 oz/
425 g) whole wheat
bread (strong
wholemeal) flour, plus
extra for dusting

2 ½ teaspoons active
dry (fast-action) yeast

1 teaspoon salt

3 tablespoons olive oil,
plus extra for greasing

milk, for brushing

FOR THE FILLING

1 tablespoon olive oil

1 onion, chopped

2 garlic cloves, finely
chopped

7 cups (7 oz/200 g)
spinach, well washed
and coarsely chopped

juice of ½ lemon

2 tablespoons pine nuts,
toasted

handful chopped mint

5 oz/150 g feta cheese,
crumbled

salt and pepper

Spinach and feta pastries

**This classic combination of spinach, pine nuts, and feta
combines with soft, just-risen dough to make melt-in-the
mouth triangular pastries. They're best eaten on the day
of baking.**

Preparation time: 45 minutes + 1 hour rising time
Cooking time: 15–20 minutes
Makes: 16

For the dough, sift the flour into a bowl. Make a well in the middle
and add the yeast to one side and the salt to the other. Pour in
the olive oil, then gradually add 1 cup (8 fl oz/250 ml) lukewarm
water and mix with a knife to bring together to form a dough.

Knead on a floured work surface for 10 minutes, until the
dough is smooth and elastic. Put the dough in a lightly oiled bowl,
cover with a dish cloth, and let rise in a warm place for about
1 hour.

Meanwhile, make the filling. Heat the oil in a skillet or frying
pan and cook the onion for 5 minutes, or until soft but not
colored. Add the garlic and cook for 1 minute. Transfer the onion
mixture into a large bowl and add the spinach, lemon juice, pine
nuts, mint, and feta. Mix together gently and season with salt
and pepper.

Preheat the oven to 400°F/200°C/Gas Mark 6 and line
2 baking sheets with parchment (baking) paper.

Return to the dough and punch down (knock back) for a few
minutes on a lightly floured work surface. Divide into 16 equal
balls the size of golf balls. Roll each ball out into 6-inch/15-cm
circles and divide the filling among each one, about one tablespoon
per pastry. Brush the edge of the dough with a little water and
then bring the dough up to form a pyramid shape (see photo).
Press the edges of the dough together with your fingers to seal.

Place the pastries on the prepared baking sheets and brush
each one with a little milk. Bake for 15–20 minutes, or until
golden. Let cool on a wire rack before serving.

Ⅴ Replace the feta cheese with firm tofu.

1. Fava bean and mint falafel 2. Labneh 2. Shanklish cheese with za'atar and paprika 3. Zucchini kibbeh

③

⑤

④

4. Grandma's eggplant dip 5. Classic hummus

Fava bean and mint falafel

These delicious falafel are very refreshing with the addition of scallion (spring onion) and mint and go perfectly with the Minted Cucumber Salad (page 120).

Preparation time: 30 minutes + overnight soaking and chilling time
Cooking time: 30 minutes
Makes: 20 falafel

Put the chickpeas and fava (broad) beans into a bowl. Pour enough hot water over them to cover, then stir in the baking soda (bicarbonate of soda) and let soak overnight.

In the morning, rinse the chickpeas and beans well. Transfer to a food processor and add the flour, garlic, scallions (spring onions), mint, cumin, dried mint, salt, and pepper. Pulse until smooth. Transfer to a dish and press down with the back of a spoon so it's flat. Cover and place in the refrigerator for a few hours to chill.

Using a falafel scoop, make 20 falafel, rinsing the scoop each time with hot water. If you don't have a scoop, take walnut-size pieces of the mixture and shape them into small oval patties with damp hands.

Pour sunflower oil into a saucepan to a depth of about 4 inches/ 10 cm. Heat to 350°F/180°C and carefully fry the falafel in batches for 1–2 minutes, until golden. Make sure the oil is back up to temperature between batches. Remove with a slotted spoon and drain on paper towels. Serve hot.

Ⓥ Ⓖ

½ cup (3 ½ oz/100 g) dried chickpeas

⅔ cup (3 ½ oz/100 g) peeled dried fava (broad) beans

½ teaspoon baking soda (bicarbonate of soda)

2 tablespoons chickpea (gram) flour

2 garlic cloves, chopped

2 scallions (spring onions), chopped

3 tablespoons chopped mint

1 tablespoon ground cumin

1 teaspoon dried mint

½ teaspoon salt

½ teaspoon pepper

sunflower oil, for frying

See pages 104–105 for photo

Classic hummus

Ⓥ Ⓖ

2 (14-oz/400-g) cans
chickpeas

3 garlic cloves, coarsely
chopped

4 tablespoons Tahini
(page 24)

juice of 2 lemons

2 teaspoons sea salt

extra-virgin olive oil,
for drizzling

Recipes for this classic dip vary around the world, but this one, which I have used for decades, is difficult to beat. I know that fresh is usually best, but I always recommend canned chickpeas for the best results with this recipe. Hummus is what I call real fast food: quick to make and easy to eat.

Preparation time: 5 minutes
Serves: 6

Drain the chickpeas, reserving scant ¼ cup (2 fl oz/50 ml) of liquid from the can. Put the chickpeas and liquid into a food processor with all the other ingredients and process until smooth. Add extra lemon juice according to taste.

Transfer into a dish and serve with a good drizzle of olive oil.

Shanklish cheese with za'atar and paprika

Ⓖ

1 quantity Lebneh
(page 25)

2 teaspoons paprika

5 tablespoons Za'atar
(page 27)

½ teaspoon chili flakes

salt

Arabic Flatbread
(page 72), to serve

This is a traditional Lebanese cheese, rolled in a warming spice blend. Not for the faint-hearted, it has a strong and rounded flavor. It is absolutely delicious when served alongside very fresh dishes, such as tabbouleh.

Preparation time: 15 minutes, plus draining time
Cooking time: 15 minutes
Makes: 6 balls

Put the lebneh into a saucepan over low heat and add 1 cup (8 fl oz/250 ml) cold water. Stir once and heat until the whey separates from the curds; this will take about 15 minutes.

Line a strainer (sieve) with a double layer of cheesecloth (muslin) and set over a bowl. Spoon the lebneh into it and let drain for about 2 hours, or until the cheese becomes dry.

Transfer the cheese to a bowl, add 1 teaspoon paprika, and season with plenty of salt. Stir well. Mix together the remaining paprika, za'atar, and chili in a shallow dish.

Then with clean wet hands, take a golf-ball-size piece of cheese and shape it into a smooth ball. Carefully roll the ball in the spice mix to coat. Repeat this with the remaining cheeses and spice mixture. Put the balls on a tray lined with parchment (baking) paper and chill in the refrigerator until set. Serve with warm flatbread.

See pages 104–105 for photo

generous 1 cup (9 oz/
250 g) dried chickpeas

4–5 potatoes, peeled and
chopped

2 tablespoons olive oil,
plus extra for greasing

2 zucchini (courgettes)

1 cup (4 ½ oz/125 g) all-
purpose (plain) flour

1 ¾ cups
(9 oz/250 g) fine bulgur
wheat

1 small bunch cilantro
(coriander), leaves
chopped

1 small bunch parsley,
leaves chopped

1 teaspoon pepper

salt

Zucchini kibbeh

This zucchini (courgette) kibbeh is a fresh green color from the herbs and zucchini and is delicious when served with a refreshing Spinach Fattoush (page 125) or dipped into Classic Hummus (page 107). Alternatively, serve with a dip such as Grandma's Eggplant Dip (page 109) or simply Tahini (page 24) with garlic and salt.

Preparation time: 45 minutes + overnight soaking time
Cooking time: 1 hour
Serves: 10–12

Put the chickpeas into a bowl. Pour enough over hot water over them to cover, then stir in the baking soda (bicarbonate of soda) and let soak overnight.

Drain the chickpeas and transfer to a clean dish cloth. Roll with a rolling pin to release the skins, pick them out, and discard.

Boil the potatoes for 20 minutes, or until tender, then mash them to a smooth consistency with about 2 tablespoons oil. Add the chickpeas to the mixture and mash in until nearly smooth.

When the mixture has cooled slightly, grate the zucchini (courgette) into the mixture and add the flour.

Preheat the oven to 350°F/180°C/Gas Mark 4 and grease a 12-inch/30-cm springform cake pan with a little oil.

Soak the bulgur wheat in plenty of cold water for 5–10 minutes. Drain well and squeeze very dry before adding it to the mixture. Add the chopped cilantro (coriander) and parsley, together with the pepper and salt to taste, and mix well using your hands.

Press the mixture into the prepared pan. Score the surface into 10–12 portions and score each portion in a crisscross pattern. Use the end of a wooden spoon or your finger to make a ¾-inch/2-cm hole in the center. Bake for 1 hour, then remove from the oven and let cool before cutting.

See pages 104–105 for photo

2 eggplants (aubergines)

2 garlic cloves, coarsely chopped

pinch of sea salt

juice of ½ small lemon

4 tablespoons extra-virgin olive oil

1 teaspoon pine nuts, toasted

Grandma's eggplant dip

I love cooking with eggplant (aubergine) and this recipe—which I learned from my grandmother when I was young—is one of my favorites. The eggplant is scorched over an open flame to bring out its maximum flavor and, as a result, this dip has a wonderful smoky taste.

Preparation time: 5 minutes
Cooking time: 20 minutes
Serves: 4

Push an all-metal fork into the stems of the eggplants (aubergines) and place them directly onto a high gas flame on your stove. Turn occasionally until they are completely soft and collapsed— the skins should be blackened all over.

When cool enough to handle, chop off the stems of the eggplants and peel off the charred skin. Do not be tempted to run them under water, because you will lose the smoky flavor. Squeeze out any excess water.

Alternatively, if you don't have a gas stove, preheat your oven to 400°F/200°C/Gas Mark 6. Put the eggplants onto a baking sheet and prick them all over with a fork. Roast in the oven for 30 minutes, or until very soft. Once they are cool enough to handle, remove the stems, peel away and discard the skin, and let the flesh cool completely.

Put the eggplant flesh into a food processor with the garlic, salt, lemon juice, and 2 tablespoons of the olive oil and blend to a smooth puree. Transfer into a serving dish, then drizzle with the rest of the oil and sprinkle with the pine nuts.

See pages 104–105 for photo

Ⓥ Ⓖ

generous 1 cup
(7 oz/200 g) dried
chickpeas

1 teaspoon baking soda
(bicarbonate of soda)

3 garlic cloves, peeled

1 small onion, chopped

1 tablespoon fresh
cilantro (coriander)

1 tablespoon fresh
parsley

1 tablespoon ground
cumin

½ teaspoon pepper

½ teaspoon salt

1 teaspoon dried mint

1 teaspoon ground
coriander

vegetable oil, for frying

1 quantity Tahini
(page 37)

Classic falafel

A mezze just doesn't seem complete without falafel. I have used the same ingredients for as long as I can remember, though the food processor certainly makes things easier than when I first made them...

Preparation time: 15 minutes + plus soaking overnight
and resting time
Cooking time: 30 minutes
Makes: 20 falafel

Soak the chickpeas overnight with ½ teaspoon of baking soda (bicarbonate of soda).

Drain the chickpeas well and discard any skins. Put the chickpeas, 2 cloves garlic, onion, cilantro (coriander), parsley, cumin, pepper, salt, mint, ground coriander, and remaining ½ teaspoon baking soda into a food processor and process until smooth and thoroughly combined. Transfer the mixture to a dish and press down with the back of a spoon. Cover with plastic wrap (clingfilm) and chill in the refrigerator for a few hours or overnight.

Using a falafel scoop, make 20 falafel, rinsing the scoop each time with hot water. If you don't have a scoop, take walnut-sized pieces of the mixture and shape them into small oval patties with damp hands.

Grate the remaining garlic clove. In a small bowl, combine the tahini and grated garlic clove, then season with salt and set aside.

Pour vegetable oil into a saucepan to a depth of 4 inches/ 10 cm. Heat the oil to 350°F/180°C, or until a cube of bread browns in 30 seconds. Carefully fry the falafel in batches for 1–2 minutes, until golden. Make sure the oil is back up to temperature between batches. Remove with a slotted spoon and drain on paper towels. Serve hot and drizzle with the tahini sauce.

V

FOR THE SHELL

3 potatoes, peeled and
finely diced

1 cup (7 oz/200 g) farina
(coarse semolina)

1 ½ cups (11 oz/300 g) fine
bulgur wheat

small bunch parsley, leaves
chopped

small bunch cilantro
(coriander), leaves chopped

1 onion, finely chopped

½ teaspoon pepper

1 teaspoon ground cumin

1 teaspoon Lebanese 7-Spice
Seasoning (page 26)

vegetable oil, for deep-frying

FOR THE STUFFING

1 tablespoon olive oil

1 onion, finely chopped

¼ teaspoon pepper

¼ teaspoon Lebanese 7-Spice
Seasoning (page 26)

2 small potatoes, peeled and
finely diced

⅓ cup (2 oz/50 g) pine nuts

sea salt

FOR THE SAUCE

1 onion, finely chopped

3 cloves garlic, chopped

olive oil, for frying

½ teaspoon ground cumin

1 teaspoon salt

½ teaspoon pepper

1 tablespoon all-purpose
(plain) flour

3 ½ oz/100 g Tomato Paste
(Puree) (page 27)

Little Damascus kibbeh with pine nuts

My grandchildren love this version of kibbeh, which comes in the shape of ovals with pointed tips at each end. The outer shell is crispy, and the inside has a softer consistency, almost like a stuffing.

Preparation time: 50 minutes + 30 minutes resting and chilling
Cooking time: 30–40 minutes
Makes: 12 kibbeh

For the kibbeh shell, boil the potatoes in salted water until tender. Drain, then return to the saucepan over low heat to dry them out. Mash and season well, then let cool until easy to handle.

In a bowl, combine the farina (coarse semolina) and enough lukewarm water to just cover it and soak for 20 minutes. Rinse the bulgur wheat. Drain both in fine strainer (sieve).

Combine all the kibbeh shell ingredients, except the oil, into a bowl and mix with your hands to bring everything together like a dough. Cover and put in the refrigerator for 30 minutes to rest.

To make the stuffing, heat the oil in a skillet or frying pan over medium heat and sauté the onion for 10–12 minutes, until softened. Stir in the pepper and spice, then add the potatoes and pine nuts, season well, and cook over medium heat for 15–20 minutes, until just cooked. Stir occasionally.

Take golf-ball portions of the chilled kibbeh shell mixture and use your hands form a lemon-shape oval. Push a finger into the ball (not right through) to form a hole through the middle and fill with a teaspoon of the stuffing. Seal the hole with a pinch. Or, flatten the mixture into a disk, then mold it around a teaspoon of the filling using wet hands. Repeat with the rest of the mixture to make 12 kibbeh. The kibbeh can be frozen at this stage (defrost thoroughly before cooking).

Pour vegetable oil into a large, deep saucepan to 1 ½–2 inches/ 4–5 cm and set over medium heat. For best results, deep-fry the kibbeh at 325–350°F/170–180°C for 5–8 minutes, or until golden brown. If you don't have a thermometer, drop a little of mixture in and check that it browns and rises to the surface. Use a slotted spoon to carefully lower the kibbeh into the oil and cook in small batches of 4–5 at a time. Drain on paper towels and keep warm.

To make the sauce, cook the onion and garlic in a little olive oil over medium heat for 10–12 minutes. Add the cumin, salt, pepper, and flour, followed by the tomato paste (puree) and scant 2 cups (7 oz/200 ml) water. Simmer for 10 minutes, or until slightly thickened. Transfer the kibbeh into the sauce and serve in bowls.

Ⓖ Replace the flour with a gluten-free flour blend.

1 ¾ cups (14 oz/400 g) dried chickpeas

1 teaspoon baking soda (bicarbonate of soda)

1 tablespoon olive oil, plus extra for greasing

6 potatoes, unpeeled

2 cups (12 oz/350 g) fine bulgur wheat, soaked in water for 10 minutes

1 onion, grated

1 ¾ cups (7 ¾ oz/225 g) all-purpose (plain) flour

2 teaspoons apple pie (mixed) spice

2 teaspoons ground cumin

pinch of chili powder

1 teaspoon dried mint

salt and pepper

Chickpea kibbeh

Kibbeh, another popular Lebanese mezze dish, often comes in the form of balls or ovals with gently pointed ends. Another version is more like a sheet cake (tray bake) in that it comes out in flat slices, whether from a rectangular or round tray. With chickpea kibbeh, my preference is for this flat slice version rather than the balls, because it makes a striking contrast to falafel when they are presented together. I love that it is slightly crunchier throughout when made this way. It can be served with a dip like Avocado Tahini Dip (page 99) or simply some Tahini (page 24) and a little salt and garlic.

Preparation time: 20 minutes + soaking overnight
Cooking time: 2 hours
Serves: 12

Put the chickpeas into a bowl. Pour enough over hot water over them to cover, then stir in the baking soda (bicarbonate of soda) and let soak overnight.

Drain the chickpeas and transfer to a clean dish cloth. Roll with a rolling pin to release the skins, pick them out, and discard.

Preheat the oven to 425°F/220°C/Gas Mark 7. Grease a 12-inch/30-cm round cake pan with a little oil.

Bake the potatoes for 1 hour, or until the centers are soft. When cool enough to handle, cut them in half and scoop out the flesh. Put it into a bowl and mash with salt and pepper.

Drain the bulgur wheat and squeeze out any excess water. Add to the potatoes, along with the chickpeas, grated onion, flour, spices, and dried mint. Season with salt and pepper again and mix to combine. Add the olive oil to the mixture.

Press the potato-and-chickpea mixture into the prepared pan. Score the surface into 8 portions and score each portion in a crisscross pattern. Use the end of a wooden spoon or your finger to make a ¾-inch/2-cm hole in the center. Bake for 1 hour, then remove from the oven and let cool before cutting.

Salads

Ⓖ

4 raw beets (beetroot),
stems removed

3 ½ oz/100 g Lebneh
(page 25)

salt

FOR THE DRESSING

handful mint leaves

3 tablespoons olive oil

zest and juice of
1 lemon

salt and pepper

sumac, to sprinkle

Beets with lebneh and mint

A very simple dish of complementary flavors that looks stunning as an appetizer.

Preparation time: 15 minutes
Cooking time: 1–1 ¼ hours
Serves: 2 as a side dish

Preheat the oven to 375°F/190°C/Gas Mark 5.

Wash the beets (beetroot) under cold water and sprinkle with salt, then wrap each one in aluminum foil and place on a baking sheet. Roast for 1 hour, then let cool slightly before unwrapping the beets and removing the skins.

Slice the beets thinly and arrange on a plate so the slices overlap. Top with pieces of lebneh and mint leaves.

To make a dressing, mix the olive oil with the lemon juice and zest and season with salt and pepper. Pour the dressing over the salad and, finally, sprinkle the sumac over the top. Serve immediately.

Ⅴ Substitute Classic Hummus (page 107) for the lebneh.

3 cucumbers

handful mint leaves,
finely chopped, plus
extra to garnish

1 garlic clove, minced

3 tablespoons plain
(natural) yogurt

salt and pepper

Minted cucumber salad

Some dishes, in all their simplicity, become instant classics, and this is one of them. The cooling properties of the cucumber and mint join forces to make a refreshing salad that is perfect for warmer days.

Preparation time: 5 minutes
Serves: 4

Cut the cucumber into small cubes and put into a bowl. Add the chopped mint and garlic, then pour in the yogurt. Mix well, season to taste with salt and pepper, and transfer to a serving plate. Sprinkle with mint leaves and serve immediately.

Ⓥ Replace the yogurt with unsweetened soy yogurt.

1 tablespoon coriander
seeds

1 teaspoon cumin seeds

2 eggplants (aubergines),
peeled and cut into
large chunks

2 tablespoons olive oil,
plus extra for frying

2 garlic cloves, crushed

gluten-free flour, for
dusting

⅔ cup (3 ½ oz/100 g)
pine nuts

1 bunch parsley, leaves
coarsely chopped

handful baby spinach
leaves, chopped

handful pomegranate
seeds

salt and pepper

FOR THE DRESSING

4 tablespoons
pomegranate juice

1 teaspoon balsamic
vinegar

juice ½ lemon

4 tablespoons olive oil

salt and pepper

Eggplant and pomegranate salad with toasted pine nuts

Meaty eggplant (aubergine) and sweet-and-sour pomegranate make a delicious pair here, with toasted pine nuts offering a finishing crunch.

Preparation time: 20 minutes
Cooking time: 30 minutes
Serves: 4

Preheat the oven to 400°F/200°C/Gas Mark 6.

Put the coriander and cumin seeds into a mortar and crush them with a pestle. Toast them in a dry skillet or frying pan for a few minutes, or until fragrant.

Put the eggplants (aubergines) into a large bowl and toss with the olive oil, crushed garlic, salt, and pepper. Sprinkle on the toasted coriander and cumin seeds.

Drizzle 1 tablespoon oil onto a baking sheet. Dip the eggplants lightly in the flour. Place them on the baking sheet and roast for 30 minutes, or until chargrilled and slightly crisp. Let cool.

While the eggplants are roasting, mix all the dressing ingredients together and set aside.

Put the roasted eggplants into a bowl, pour 1–2 tablespoons of the dressing, and toss well. Let stand for 10 minutes so the dressing can absorb.

Heat 2 teaspoon olive oil in a skillet or frying pan and lightly toast the pine nuts until golden.

Add the chopped parsley, spinach, and pomegranate seeds to the eggplants and toss together well. Sprinkle on the toasted pine nuts and serve with the remaining dressing.

V

1 Arabic Flatbread
(page 72)

7 cups (7 oz/200 g) baby
spinach, washed

2 scallions (spring
onions), cut into thin
strips

1 teaspoon Lebanese
7-Spice Seasoning
(page 26)

1 garlic clove, crushed

juice of 1 lemon

4 tablespoons olive oil

salt and pepper

Spinach fattoush

Another version of fattoush, this time with spinach and a fresh bite from the scallions (spring onions).

Preparation time: 5 minutes, plus cooling time
Cooking time: 2 minutes
Serves: 4

Toast the flatbread under a hot broiler (grill) until golden and crisp. Set aside to cool, then break into bite-size pieces.

Put the spinach into a large bowl, then add the scallions (spring onions).

Mix the 7-spice seasoning with the crushed garlic, lemon juice, and olive oil and pour over the spinach salad. Season with salt and pepper and toss all the ingredients together. Finally, add the crisp, toasted bread and serve.

scant 1 cup (7 oz/200 g)
cracked or wholegrain
freekeh, rinsed

pinch of sea salt

4 tablespoons olive oil

2 tablespoons
pomegranate molasses

1 small bunch mint,
leaves coarsely chopped

1 small bunch parsley,
leaves coarsely chopped

1 1/3 cups (5 oz/150 g)
coarsely chopped
walnuts

7 oz/200 g feta cheese,
crumbled

seeds from
1 pomegranate (around
3 ½ oz/100 g)

salt

Freekeh, pomegranate, and feta salad

Freekeh (pronounced "free-ka") is an ancient grain, native to Lebanon, Jordan, Syria, and Egypt. The wheat is harvested when not quite ripe and still slightly green. It has a nutty flavor that goes beautifully with the sweet pomegranate and refreshing mint in this salad. It is available as a "quick-cook" grain, too; check the package instructions for cooking times.

Preparation time: 10 minutes
Cooking time: 10–45 minutes
Serves: 4–6

Put the freekeh in a saucepan with 1 ⅔ cups (14 fl oz/400 ml) cold water, salt, and 1 tablespoon of the olive oil. Cover with a lid and bring to a boil over medium heat. Turn the heat down to a simmer and cook until the grains become tender, adding more water, if necessary. This will take about 10 minutes for cracked freekeh and up to 45 minutes for wholegrain freekeh.

When cooked, drain off any excess water and let the freekeh cool.

To make the dressing, combine 3 tablespoons of olive oil, the pomegranate molasses, half of the chopped mint and parsley, and salt. Mix well.

In a separate bowl, combine the freekeh, rest of the chopped herbs, walnuts, feta, and pomegranate seeds and mix well. Pour over the dressing and toss together.

V Omit the feta and replace with jarred roasted red peppers.

1. Chickpea and freekeh salad 2. Carrots, cilantro, and sesame Seeds 3. Fennel and celery root slaw with sumac

4. Garlicky bean and lemon salad 5. Okra with pearl barley

generous 1 cup (9 oz/
250 g) cracked or
whole-grain freekeh,
rinsed

3 tablespoons extra-
virgin olive oil, plus
extra to drizzle

2 eggplants (aubergines)

4 garlic cloves, crushed

small bunch parsley,
leaves chopped

small bunch mint,
leaves chopped

1 (14-oz/400-g) can
chickpeas, drained and
rinsed

handful sun-dried
tomatoes in oil

salt and pepper

Chickpea and freekeh salad

**The sun-dried tomatoes and mint provide a delicately sweet
and refreshing flavor to this salad. I enjoy it when dining
al fresco. It's a simple but flavorsome and substantial salad.**

Preparation time: 15 minutes
Cooking time: 30–40 minutes
Serves: 4

Put the freekeh in a saucepan, with a generous 2 cups (17 fl oz/
500 ml) cold water, a pinch of salt, and 1 tablespoon of olive oil.
Cover and bring to a boil over medium heat. Turn the heat down
to a simmer and cook until the grains become tender, adding more
water, if necessary. This will take about 10 minutes for cracked
freekeh and up to 45 minutes for whole-grain freekeh.

While the freekeh is cooking, preheat the oven to 350°F/180°C/
Gas Mark 4.

Slice the eggplants (aubergines) lengthwise into ½-inch/1-cm
slices and place on a baking sheet, skin side down. Score the flesh
and sprinkle with a good pinch of salt and pepper. Spread the
garlic onto the eggplant slices and drizzle on a little oil. Roast for
30 minutes, until soft and golden.

When the freekeh is cooked, drain off any excess water and
let cool.

Transfer the freekeh to a large bowl and add the roasted
eggplant, herbs, chickpeas, and sun-dried tomatoes. Add the
remaining 2 tablespoons of olive oil—or use oil from the sun-
dried tomatoes instead for greater flavor. Season well and serve.

See pages 128–129 for photo

Ⓥ Ⓖ

1 lb 2 oz/500 g carrots,
cut into sticks

1 tablespoon olive oil

handful cilantro
(coriander) leaves

1 tablespoon toasted
sesame seeds

ground pink Himalayan
salt and pepper

Ⓖ

1 fennel bulb, thinly
sliced

½ celery root (celeriac),
peeled, thinly sliced and
cut into matchsticks

1 large carrot, peeled
and grated

FOR THE DRESSING

2 tablespoons plain
(natural) yogurt

1 tablespoon chopped
chives

handful chopped parsley
leaves

juice of 1 lemon

½ teaspoon Dijon or
English mustard

1 teaspoon sumac, plus
extra to serve

salt and pepper

Carrots, cilantro, and sesame seeds

This classic flavor combination is as much about texture as taste. It is best served hot but it is also nice the next day as a cold salad. The cilantro can be chopped, if desired.

Preparation time: 10 minutes
Cooking time: 15–20 minutes
Serves: 4 (as a side)

Preheat the oven to 400°F/200°C/Gas Mark 6.

Put the carrot sticks into a bowl, toss with olive oil, and sprinkle with salt. Transfer the carrots to a roasting pan and roast for 15–20 minutes, or until tender.

Toss the carrots in the cilantro (coriander) and sesame seeds and season well with salt and pepper.

Fennel and celery root slaw with sumac

A light, fresh, and zesty salad bound with yogurt. It makes the perfect accompaniment to a vegetable burger or can be stuffed inside a Pita Bread (page 70) with a few falafel for a delicious and satisfying lunch.

Preparation time: 10 minutes
Serves: 4

To make the dressing, combine the yogurt with all the remaining ingredients and mix well.

Put the fennel, celery root (celeriac), and carrots into a mixing bowl. Toss with the dressing and serve immediately, or store in an airtight container in the refrigerator for a few days. Sprinkle with a little extra sumac to serve.

Ⓥ Replace the yogurt with unsweetened soy yogurt.

See pages 128–129 for photo

V G

14 oz/400 g runner or
string beans, sliced into
1 ¼-inch/3-cm pieces

4 garlic cloves

juice of 1 ½ lemons

3 tablespoons olive oil
sea salt

Garlicky bean and lemon salad

**Garlic and lemon bring out the best flavor of runner beans.
The combination is simple but tastes absolutely delicious and
makes for a great side dish.**

Preparation time: 5 minutes
Cooking time: 4–5 minutes
Serves: 4

Cook the beans in boiling salted water for a few minutes, or until
just tender. Drain them and set aside in a serving bowl.

Put the garlic with the salt and lemon juice into a mortar and
crush with a pestle. Add the olive oil and mix together well to
make a dressing.

Pour onto the beans, toss well, and serve immediately.

See pages 128–129 for photo

Ⓥ Ⓖ

1 lb 2 oz/500 g okra,
washed, trimmed,
and dried

3 garlic cloves

2 tablespoons olive oil

1 ¾ cups (9 oz/250 g)
cherry tomatoes

½ cup (3 ½ oz/100 g)
pearl barley, rinsed

juice of 1 lemon

1 tablespoon extra-
virgin olive oil

¼ cup (1 oz/30 g)
toasted pine nuts

1 bunch parsley, leaves
chopped

salt and pepper

Okra with pearl barley and tomato

I always describe this dish as the ultimate Middle Eastern comfort food. It has a rich garlic and tomato sauce that I love.

Preparation time: 10 minutes
Cooking time: 25 minutes
Serves: 6

Preheat the oven to 375°F/190°C/Gas Mark 5.

Arrange the okra and garlic cloves on a baking sheet. Drizzle with the olive oil, then toss and season with salt and pepper. Roast for 10 minutes, then add the tomatoes and roast for another 15 minutes.

Meanwhile, cook the pearl barley in 1 ¼ cups (10 fl oz/300 ml) water for 25 minutes, or until tender with a little bite, topping up with more water, if necessary. When cooked, drain off any excess water and let cool.

Transfer the pearl barley to a large bowl and mix with the roasted okra and cherry tomatoes.

Combine the lemon juice with the extra-virgin olive oil, then pour onto the salad. Toss well and top with the toasted pine nuts and chopped parsley.

See pages 128–129 for photo

1 ⅔ cups (14 oz/400 g)
fresh or frozen fava
(broad) beans

1 cup (7 oz/200 g) raw
or toasted buckwheat

1 ⅔ cups (14 fl oz/
400 ml) vegetable broth
(stock) or water

1 ⅓ cups (5 oz/150 g)
chopped walnuts

1 bunch radishes,
quartered

1 small bunch scallions
(spring onions), finely
sliced

Arabic Flatbread
(page 72), to serve

FOR THE DRESSING

1 tablespoon white wine
vinegar

3 tablespoons walnut oil

1 tablespoon olive oil

1 small bunch parsley,
leaves finely chopped

salt and pepper

Buckwheat and fava bean salad

The grainlike seeds of buckwheat make for a light and incredibly fresh-tasting salad. I like to add radishes, walnuts, and fava (broad) beans for plenty of texture. Raw buckwheat groats take longer to cook than the toasted seeds I normally use, but both are equally delicious.

Preparation time: 20 minutes
Cooking time: 15–20 minutes
Serves: 4

Put the broad (fava) beans into a saucepan and cover with boiling water. Return to a simmer, cover, and cook for 2–4 minutes, or until tender.

Plunge the beans into cold water, then pop them out of their outer skins.

If using raw buckwheat, rinse under cold water and check the package for any presoak instructions. Combine the buckwheat and broth (stock) or water in a saucepan and bring to a boil. Lower the heat and simmer for 15–20 minutes for toasted buckwheat, or nearer 30 minutes for raw groats, until the seeds are tender but retaining a little bite. Drain away any remaining water.

Meanwhile, toast the walnuts in a dry skillet or frying pan until slightly golden.

Whisk together the ingredients for the dressing.

Transfer the buckwheat into a mixing bowl and add the fava (broad) beans, radishes, walnuts, and scallions (spring onions). Stir through the dressing and serve, while still warm, with flatbread.

Note: Though vegetable stock brings a depth of flavor to the dish; generally, I cook my grains in water.

2 Boston, Little Gem, or other small butterhead lettuce, chopped

1 large bunch parsley, leaves finely chopped

1 bunch mint, leaves finely chopped

½ cucumber, cubed

1 ¾ cups (9 oz/250 g) cherry tomatoes, halved

4 scallions (spring onions), finely chopped

juice of 1 lemon

1 teaspoon apple cider vinegar

scant ½ cup (3 ½ fl oz/ 100 ml) olive oil, plus extra for frying

1 garlic clove, crushed

1 tablespoon sumac

1 Arabic Flatbread (page 72), cut into ½-inch/ 1-cm square pieces

salt and pepper

Fattoush

Another classic Middle Eastern dish, fattoush is traditionally made with stale bread. A small bowl of salad, such as this, is often served with lunch or supper in Lebanon.

Preparation time: 15 minutes
Cooking time: 2 minutes (to toast the bread)
Serves: 4

In a large bowl, mix together the chopped lettuce, herbs, cucumber, tomatoes, and scallions (spring onions) and put to one side.

In a small bowl, lightly whisk the lemon juice with the vinegar, olive oil, garlic, and sumac. Season with salt and pepper.

Heat a little oil in a skillet or frying pan and fry the pieces of flatbread with a little salt until golden. Add the bread to the bowl. Pour over the dressing and mix well to combine. Remove the garlic clove and serve immediately.

Ⓖ Substitute the flatbread for a gluten-free option.

Ⓥ Ⓖ

3 sweet potatoes, peeled and cut into wedges

1 teaspoon cumin seeds

1 tablespoon olive oil

1 cup (7 oz/200 g) quinoa, washed

1 teaspoon ground cumin

4 scallions (spring onions), sliced

⅓ cup (2 oz/50 g) chopped walnuts

handful chopped cilantro (coriander) leaves

salt and pepper

FOR THE DRESSING

½ cup (2 ¼ oz/ 60 g) finely chopped walnuts

2 tablespoons olive oil, plus more if needed

1 tablespoon water

2 garlic cloves

juice of 1 lemon

1 teaspoon white wine vinegar

salt and pepper

Sweet potatoes with walnuts and quinoa

A hearty dish with plenty of flavor and texture. I find that the creamy walnut dressing gives a wonderful, nutty texture to the quinoa.

Preparation time: 15 minutes
Cooking time: 20–25 minutes
Serves: 4

Preheat the oven to 375°F/190°C/Gas Mark 5.

Put the sweet potato wedges into a bowl and toss with the cumin seeds, olive oil, salt and pepper. Transfer to a baking sheet and roast for 20–25 minutes, or until they are soft and slightly charred on the edges.

Meanwhile, cook the quinoa with the ground cumin in 1 ⅔ cups (14 oz/400 ml) water for about 12 minutes, or until all the water has been absorbed and the quinoa is tender. Drain and squeeze out any excess water then set aside.

Blend all of the dressing ingredients together in a blender until loose enough to coat the quinoa, adding a little more oil if needed.

Combine the quinoa, sweet potatoes, scallions (spring onions), and walnuts and toss together. Drizzle with the dressing, season with salt and pepper, and sprinkle the chopped cilantro (coriander) over the top.

Ⓥ Ⓖ

1 butternut squash,
skin removed if desired

olive oil

FOR THE DRESSING

⅓ cup (2 ¾ oz/70 g)
Tahini (page 24)

juice of 1 lemon

1 teaspoon olive oil

3 garlic cloves, chopped

1 red chile, seeded and
finely chopped

½ teaspoon chili
powder, plus extra to
garnish

½ teaspoon cayenne
pepper

3 tablespoons toasted
pine nuts

2 tablespoons chopped
walnuts

1 small bunch cilantro
(coriander),
leaves chopped

Roasted butternut squash with spicy tahini dressing

This dish always tends to disappear soon after bringing it out! Drizzle the dressing over the slices of squash or serve it on the side in a small bowl for dipping into.

Preparation time: 5 minutes
Cooking time: 30–35 minutes
Serves: 4

Preheat the oven to 375°F/190°C/Gas Mark 5.

Slice the squash lengthwise down the center and cut each half into ½-inch/1-cm slices. Make sure all the seeds are removed. Arrange the slices on a baking sheet, drizzle with a little olive oil, and roast for 40 minutes, or until tender, turning so both sides cook evenly.

To make the dressing, combine the tahini and lemon juice in a bowl and whisk with 6 tablespoons of water to a smooth paste.

Heat the oil in a skillet or frying pan, then add the garlic, chopped chile, chili powder, and cayenne pepper, and cook for 1 minute. Add the pine nuts, walnuts, and tahini mixture and cook, stirring for 1–2 minutes, or until the sauce thickens. Remove the pan from the heat and stir in the chopped cilantro (coriander).

Arrange the warm slices of squash on a serving plate and serve with the hot sauce on the side or drizzled on as a dressing. Sprinkle with a little chili powder.

Ⓥ Ⓖ

1 cauliflower (about 1 lb
4 oz/550 g), cut into
florets

1 tablespoon olive oil

1 teaspoon Lebanese
7-Spice Seasoning
(page 26)

½ teaspoon cumin
seeds, lightly crushed

FOR THE DIP

3 garlic cloves, crushed

2 tablespoons Tahini
(page 24)

1 tablespoon olive oil

juice ½ lemon

handful parsley, leaves
chopped

salt

Roasted cauliflower with garlic-tahini dip

Roasting does something magical to cauliflower, I find, and cumin complements the earthy flavor of the vegetable wonderfully.

Preparation time: 10 minutes
Cooking time: 35–40 minutes
Serves: 4

Chop any large florets in half for even cooking. Cook in boiling water for 2 minutes, or until nearly tender. Drain and let steam dry, then transfer into a bowl.

Preheat the oven to 375°F/190°C/Gas Mark 5.

Toss the cauliflower florets in the olive oil, 7-spice, and cumin seeds. Transfer the cauliflower to a baking sheet and roast for 30–40 minutes, or until crisp and golden.

For the dip, combine the garlic with a little salt in a small bowl. Add the tahini, olive oil, lemon juice, and a splash of water to make the consistency of heavy (double) cream. Mix well and then add the chopped parsley, adding more water, if necessary. Serve alongside the roasted florets for dipping.

Vegetables

½ head broccoli

2 cups (7 oz/200g) sliced
green beans, such as
Italian flat green beans
or runner beans

1 teaspoon olive oil

1 onion, chopped

2 garlic cloves, chopped

generous 1 cup
(6 oz/170 g) cherry
tomatoes

1 teaspoon dried mint

salt and pepper

Fried broccoli, beans,
and tomatoes

**This is a staple mezze dish, served as part of a big spread.
Use the best broccoli you can find; purple sprouting broccoli
is great for this dish, too.**

Preparation time: 5 minutes
Cooking time: 10–15 minutes
Serves: 4

Put the broccoli and beans into a large saucepan of salted boiling
water and boil for 2 minutes. Drain and set aside.

Heat the olive oil in a skillet or frying pan and sauté the onion
until soft. Add the garlic and fry for 1 minute. Add the broccoli,
beans, and tomatoes to the pan and cook for 5 minutes, or until
everything is tender.

Add the dried mint and season with salt and pepper.

Quinoa stuffed peppers

This dish of sweet red bell peppers with a savory chickpea and quinoa stuffing is one of my husband Heni's favorites. It is served with a Lebanese spiced tomato sauce.

Ⓥ Ⓖ

generous ½ cup
(4 oz/120 g) red or
mixed quinoa, rinsed

1 tablespoon olive oil

2 onions, chopped

1 yellow bell pepper,
seeded and diced

1 (14-oz/400-g) can
chickpeas, drained and
rinsed

1 teaspoon ground
cumin

4 red bell peppers,
seeded and halved

handful chopped parsley
leaves, to garnish

salt and pepper

FOR THE SAUCE

1 tablespoon olive oil

1 onion, chopped

⅓ cup (3 ½ oz/100 g)
Tomato Paste (Puree)
(page 27)

1 teaspoon Lebanese
7-Spice Seasoning
(page 26)

salt and pepper

Preparation time: 15 minutes
Cooking time: 1 hour
Serves: 4

Cook the quinoa in 1 cup (8 fl oz/250 ml) water for about 12 minutes, or until all the water has been absorbed and the quinoa is tender. Drain, rinse, and squeeze out any excess water, then set aside in a large bowl.

Heat the olive oil in a skillet or frying pan. Sauté the onion and yellow bell pepper together for a few minutes. Next, add the chickpeas and cumin and cook for another 5 minutes. Season well with salt and pepper, then transfer to the bowl with the quinoa and toss everything together.

Preheat the oven to 375°F/190°C/Gas Mark 5.

For the sauce, heat the oil in a saucepan, then add the onion and sauté until slightly golden. Add the tomato paste (puree) and 3 ¼ cups (28 fl oz/800 ml) of boiling water. Cook for 10 minutes on a rolling boil, then add the 7-spice and season well with salt and pepper. Pour the sauce into an ovenproof dish and set aside.

Fill the red bell pepper halves with the stuffing and carefully sink them into the sauce in the ovenproof dish. Any leftover stuffing can be added to the sauce to help it thicken. Cook for 30–35 minutes.

Remove from the oven, let cool slightly before sprinkling with parsley, and serve.

Ⓥ Ⓖ

2 tablespoons olive oil

1 onion, chopped

2 small carrots, peeled
and cubed

2 garlic cloves, crushed

1 sprig thyme

3 ½ cups (9 oz/250 g)
quartered white
mushrooms

3 cups (9 oz/250 g)
quartered cremini
(chestnut) mushrooms

6 ¼ cups (50 fl oz/
1.5 liters) vegetable
broth (stock), plus a little
more, if needed

salt and pepper

bread, to serve

FOR THE TOPPING

½ tablespoon olive oil,
plus extra for drizzling

1 heaping teaspoon
sumac

⅔ cup (3 ½ oz/100 g)
pine nuts

salt and pepper

Mushroom soup with toasted sumac pine nuts

A traditional vegetable soup with a deep, umami flavor topped with spicy toasted pine nuts.

Preparation time: 10 minutes
Cooking time: 30 minutes
Serves: 4–6

Heat 1 tablespoon of oil in a large saucepan and add the onion and carrots. Sauté gently for a couple of minutes, then add the garlic and thyme. Continue cooking until the vegetables are soft, but not colored.

Add the mushrooms and another tablespoon of oil to the pan, and cook for 10 minutes over simmering heat, stirring every few minutes. Pour in the vegetable broth (stock) and cook for 20 minutes.

Remove from the heat, discard the thyme sprig, and carefully pour into a food processor. Process until smooth, then return the soup to a clean pan and season well with salt and pepper. Adjust the consistency with more stock if necessary and keep warm until ready to serve.

To make the topping, heat the oil in a small skillet or frying pan over high heat. Add the sumac and plenty of seasoning. Add the pine nuts and toast until golden.

Ladle the soup into individual bowls, drizzle with olive oil, and sprinkle with the pine nut topping.

3 carrots, peeled and cut into sticks

2 cups (7 oz/200 g) fine green beans

½ head broccoli, cut into small florets

2 tablespoons extra-virgin olive oil

2 onions, finely chopped

4 garlic cloves, finely chopped

1 teaspoon curry powder

½ teaspoon ground cumin

½ teaspoon Lebanese 7-Spice Seasoning (page 26)

½ teaspoon pepper

1 ¼ cups (10 ½ fl oz/ 300 ml) boiling vegetable broth (stock)

2 heaping teaspoons gluten-free flour

salt

steamed rice, to serve

Pita Bread (page 70), to serve (optional)

Spiced broccoli and beans

An easy, warming blend of vegetables and spices with great strong flavors. This quick-and-easy curry is delicious when served with rice or pita bread.

Preparation time: 15 minutes
Cooking time: 15 minutes
Serves: 4

Steam or blanch the vegetables for 5–10 minutes, or until just tender. (Start with the carrots, then add the broccoli and beans a few minutes later.) Run them under cold water in a colander to stop them from cooking. The crunch of the vegetables is vital to this recipe, so don't overcook them.

Heat the oil in a saucepan on medium heat. Add the onion and garlic and sauté for 5 minutes, until soft but not brown. Add all the spices and cook for a couple of minutes, then add the vegetable broth (stock). In a separate cup, mix the flour with a little cold water to make a thin cream consistency (this will stop the flour from clumping when you add it to the liquid). Add to the pan and cook until the sauce is thick and fragrant. Season to taste.

Stir the sauce through the blanched vegetables and cook for 5 minutes, until the vegetables are cooked but retaining a little bite. Serve with rice and pita bread, if desired.

V G

1 large bunch green
asparagus, trimmed
(about 20 spears)

olive oil

1 tablespoon Za'atar
(page 27)

salt and pepper

handful slivered (flaked)
almonds, toasted

Grilled asparagus with za'atar and almonds

This Middle Eastern dish is simple yet outstandingly delicious. The za'atar pairs wonderfully with asparagus spears and the almonds add a lovely texture to finish.

Preparation time: 5 minutes
Cooking time: 10 minutes
Serves: 4

Heat a ridged grill (griddle) pan over a high heat.

Toss the asparagus spears with olive oil. Arrange them on the hot grill pan in a single layer and cook for a few minutes, turning occasionally, until they start to char. You may need to cook them in 2 batches. Sprinkle with za'atar and season generously.

Serve warm, sprinkled with the toasted almonds.

Ⓥ Ⓖ

1 butternut squash, peeled and diced

3 carrots, peeled and diced

2 sweet potatoes, peeled and diced

3 tablespoons olive oil

1 teaspoon ground cumin

4 ¼–6 ¼ cups (34–50 fl oz/1–1.5 liters) vegetable broth (stock), plus a little more if needed

4 tablespoons Za'atar (page 27), plus extra to garnish

2 tablespoons toasted sesame seeds

sea salt and pepper

Arabic Flatbread (page 72), to serve (optional)

Lebneh (page 25), to serve (optional)

Za'atar-spiced butternut squash and carrot soup

This is a simple soup, bright in color and flavor, yet tangy and sweet. In addition to the za'atar, extra toasted sesame seeds are added just before serving for a delicious crunch. I make this when I have a lot of people over for lunch, because it is easy to make, tasty, and filling.

Preparation time: 10 minutes
Cooking time: 30 minutes
Serves: 8–10

Preheat the oven to 350°F/180°C/Gas Mark 4.

Put the squash, carrots, and sweet potatoes into a large bowl and toss with the olive oil, cumin, and 1 teaspoon pepper.

Spread them out onto a baking sheet in a single layer and roast for 30–40 minutes, or until soft and yielding.

Transfer the roasted vegetables to a large saucepan over medium heat and add the vegetable broth (stock). Use an immersion (stick) blender to puree until smooth. (Alternatively, combine everything in a food processor and puree.) Add more broth if necessary, until you get a creamy soup consistency. Add the za'atar, salt, and pepper and stir well.

Serve hot with a sprinkling of za'atar, toasted sesame seeds, and bread, and lebneh, if desired.

Ⓥ Ⓖ

½ cup (3 ½ oz/100 g)
green lentils, rinsed

1 cup (8 fl oz/
250 ml) vegetable broth
(stock)

1 onion, finely chopped

1 small bunch parsley,
leaves finely chopped

8 cherry tomatoes,
quartered

2 garlic cloves, finely
chopped

juice of 1 lemon

2 tablespoons olive oil

1 teaspoon Lebanese
7-Spice Seasoning
(page 26)

1 teaspoon ground
cumin

salt and pepper

Green lentil tabbouleh

**Another play on a traditional tabbouleh recipe, this is one
I like to make with lentils. It's delicious stirred through
couscous or quinoa for something more substantial, too.**

Preparation time: 10 minutes
Cooking time: 15 minutes
Serves: 2

Cook the lentils in the vegetable stock for 10 minutes, or as
directed on the package. Add more broth (stock). if needed.
Drain well.

    Transfer to a bowl and add all the remaining ingredients.
Mix together well, season with plenty of salt and pepper, and
serve.

Zucchini quinoa with halloumi

Nutty quinoa, grilled halloumi, and fresh herbs, lifted by zesty lemon, make a beautiful fresh salad that is as delicious warm on the day you make it or as it is cold the next day.

Preparation time: 15 minutes
Cooking time: 35 minutes
Serves: 4

Preheat the oven to 350°F/180°C/Gas Mark 4.

In a large saucepan over medium-high heat, bring the vegetable broth (stock) to a boil. Add the quinoa and simmer for 12 minutes, or until tender. Drain, rinse, and squeeze out any excess water, then fluff with a fork and set aside.

Cut the zucchini (courgettes) lengthwise into 8 slices about ¼ inch/5 mm thick. Spread out on a baking sheet and drizzle with the olive oil. Season well and sprinkle with 1 teaspoon of the ground cumin. Roast for 25 minutes, or until soft, yielding, and golden.

Whisk the lemon juice and vinegar with 3 tablespoons olive oil and stir through the quinoa. Season well.

Toward the end of the zucchini cooking time, prepare the halloumi. Set an oiled grill (griddle) pan over high heat. Sprinkle the remaining cumin over the halloumi slices and cook for 3–4 minutes on each side, turning as they become golden.

To serve, stir the zucchini strips into the quinoa, along with the chopped herbs and pine nuts. Top with the hot halloumi slices, straight from the pan.

[V] Replace the halloumi with firm tofu, cut into ½-inch/1-cm strips and press on paper towels to dry. Sprinkle with cumin and season generously with salt and pepper before cooking on the grill pan.

Ⓖ

generous 2 cups
(17 fl oz/500 ml)
vegetable broth (stock)

1 ¼ cups (9 oz/250 g)
quinoa

3 cups (25 fl oz/750 ml)
vegetable broth (stock)

2 zucchini (courgettes),
trimmed

3 tablespoons extra-
virgin olive oil, plus
extra to drizzle

2 teaspoons ground
cumin

juice of ½ lemon

1 tablespoon white wine
vinegar

9 oz/250 g halloumi, cut
into 8 x ⅔ inch/1 cm
thick slices

1 small bunch mint,
leaves chopped

1 small bunch parsley,
leaves chopped

⅓ cup (2 oz/50 g)
toasted pine nuts

salt and pepper

2 ⅓ cups (11 oz/300 g) all-purpose (plain) flour, plus extra for dusting

1 stick plus 1 tablespoon (5 oz/150 g) unsalted butter, cubed, plus extra for greasing

FOR THE FILLING

1 cup (4 ½ oz/125 g) asparagus tips

1 teaspoon olive oil

1 onion, finely chopped

2 garlic cloves, crushed

3 ½ oz/100 g feta cheese, crumbled

3 extra large (UK: large) eggs, lightly beaten

1 ¼ cups (10 ½ fl oz/ 300 ml) crème fraiche

2 tablespoons fresh mint, finely chopped

salt and pepper

Asparagus and feta quiche

Every so often the French influence appears in our cooking in Lebanon, and nowhere more so than in this classic quiche.

Preparation time: 20 minutes + 30 minutes chilling
Cooking time: 25–30 minutes
Serves: 8

To make the pastry dough, put the flour and butter into a large bowl and rub them together with your fingertips until the mixture resembles fine crumbs. Add 4 tablespoons of chilled water and use a blunt kitchen knife to bring the dough together. Then use your hands to shape it into a smooth ball. Turn the dough out onto a floured surface and knead gently and briefly. Wrap in plastic wrap (clingfilm) and chill for 30 minutes.

Preheat the oven to 375°F/190°C/Gas Mark 5 and grease a 9-inch/25-cm fluted tart pan with a removable base.

Roll the chilled dough out on a lightly floured surface, then carefully transfer to the prepared pan, pressing it into the sides and trimming and discarding the edges. Prick the dough with a fork and line with parchment (baking) paper and pie weights (baking beans). Sit the pan on a baking sheet and bake blind for 12 minutes. Remove the paper and beans and bake for another 10 minutes, or until lightly golden.

To make the filling, first blanch the asparagus tips briefly in boiling water. Drain and rinse under cold water, then pat dry and set aside.

Heat the oil in a skillet or frying pan and sauté the onion until soft but not browned. Sauté the garlic and fry for 1 minute. Spread the onions and garlic over the pastry, then add the asparagus tips and feta cheese.

Whisk together the eggs and crème fraiche, add the mint, and season well with salt and pepper. Pour into the pastry shell (case), then return to the oven and bake for 25–30 minutes, or until the filling is golden and just set. Remove from the oven and let set, then slice and serve while still hot.

Ⓖ Replace the all-purpose (plain) flour with gluten-free flour.

1. Stuffed zucchini in yogurt 2. Stuffed mushrooms with lebneh and za'atar crumbs 3. Jidi potatoes 4. Eggplant and okra stew

5. Zucchini turnovers

6–8 zucchini
(courgettes)

½ cup (4 oz/120 g)
basmati rice

1 ⅔ cups (7-oz/200-g)
can chickpeas, drained,
rinsed, and coarsely
chopped

2 tomatoes, finely
chopped

½ onion, finely diced

1 garlic clove, crushed

1 small bunch parsley,
leaves finely chopped

½ teaspoon pepper

½ teaspoon Lebanese
7-Spice Seasoning
(page 26)

½ teaspoon ground
cumin

salt

fresh mint leaves, to
serve

Arabic Flatbread
(page 72), to serve

FOR THE SAUCE

2 cups (2 ¼ lb/500 g)
plain (natural) yogurt

1 egg, lightly beaten

1 tablespoon cornstarch
(cornflour)

½ teaspoon dried mint

salt and pepper

Stuffed zucchini in yogurt

Cooking zucchini (courgettes) in yogurt gives them a delicious milky flavor and I like to scoop up the sauce with plenty of bread. Don't panic if your sauce is a little grainy—the cornstarch (cornflour) should prevent this, but it will still be delicious if it separates a little.

Preparation time: 20 minutes
Cooking time: 1 hour
Serves: 6–8

Trim the tops and brown bases from the zucchini (courgettes) and cut the zucchini in half lengthwise. Use an apple corer or small knife to remove the flesh from the zucchini, leaving a ¹/₈-inch/ 3-mm shell.

Preheat the oven to 375°C/190°F/Gas Mark 5.

To make the stuffing, fill a small saucepan halfway with water. Add a little salt and bring to the boil over high heat. Add the rice, reduce the heat to a simmer, and cook according for 10 minutes, until tender. Drain in a sieve.

Combine the rice, chickpeas, tomatoes, onion, garlic, parsley, pepper, Lebanese 7-spice, cumin, and salt. Mix thoroughly and spoon the filling into six zucchini halves. Cover each with the other zucchini half. Set aside.

For the sauce, place the yogurt in a bowl and whisk in the egg, then stir in the cornstarch and the mint. Season with salt and pepper and pour into a baking dish. Gentle place each stuffed zucchini into the dish, then cover with foil.

Bake in the oven for 1 hour or until the zucchini is tender when a sharp skewer is inserted. Garnish with fresh mint and serve warm or at room temperature with Arabic flatbread.

See pages 164–165 for photo

Stuffed mushrooms with lebneh and za'atar crumbs

4 portobello mushrooms

olive oil, for drizzling

½ cup (1 oz/25 g) fresh bread crumbs

4 heaping teaspoons Za'atar (page 27), plus extra for sprinkling

4 tablespoons Lebneh (page 25)

salt and pepper

Smooth, tangy lebneh and crisp, za'atar-spiced bread crumbs top off meaty portobello mushrooms here to make a tasty and textured dish. Serve with a Fattoush Salad (page 137) for lunch, or brown rice for dinner, or simply enjoy them on their own.

Preparation time: 5 minutes
Cooking time: 20 minutes
Serves: 4

Preheat the oven to 350°F/180°C/Gas Mark 4.

Place the mushrooms on a baking sheet. Drizzle with oil and season well. Mix the fresh bread crumbs with the za'atar and spoon over each mushroom. Add a tablespoon of lebneh on top. Bake for 20 minutes, until golden. Sprinkle a little za'atar over each mushroom and serve immediately.

Ⓖ Replace fresh bread crumbs with a gluten-free option.

Jidi potatoes

Ⓥ Ⓖ

4 russet, Maris Piper, or any floury potatoes

1 onion, finely chopped

handful mint leaves, chopped

2 tablespoons extra-virgin olive oil

salt and pepper

Ever since I was a young girl, I have been cooking for my household: first alongside my mother and then later, by myself, making meals for my husband, Heni, and son, Joe.

Heni, though, has a specialty: potatoes. The grandchildren requested these ones so often that they became known as *jidi*, or "grandfather" potatoes.

Preparation time: 5 minutes
Cooking time: 1 hour
Serves: 4, as a side

Preheat the oven to 400°F/200°C/Gas Mark 6.

Prick the potatoes with a fork and bake for 1 hour, or until tender. Remove from the oven and let cool slightly.

When the potatoes are cool enough to handle, cut them in half, scoop out the flesh, and put it into a bowl. Add the onion, mint, and olive oil and season to taste with salt and pepper. Mix well until thoroughly combined.

Serve hot.

See pages 164–165 for photo

1 eggplant (aubergine),
cut into large chunks

1 teaspoon sea salt

11 oz/300 g okra

2 tablespoons olive oil

**FOR THE
TOMATO SAUCE**

1 tablespoon olive oil

1 onion, chopped

1 garlic clove, crushed

9 oz/250 g cherry
tomatoes

1 red bell pepper, seeded
and cubed

1 (14-oz/400-g) can
diced or chopped
tomatoes

1 teaspoon Lebanese
7-Spice Seasoning
(page 26)

handful parsley leaves,
chopped

salt and pepper

Eggplant and okra stew

Though the Middle East is best known for its mezzes, it also has a long history of sustaining stews. My kitchen is rarely without a huge pot of vegetables stewing away on the stove top, which fills the kitchen with fragrance from Lebanese 7-spice.

Preparation time: 10 minutes
Cooking time: 1 hour 10 minutes
Serves: 4

Preheat the oven to 375°F/190°C/Gas Mark 5.

Cut the eggplant (aubergine) into large chunks and toss with the salt. Let stand for 10 minutes and then pat dry.

Mix the eggplant with the okra and toss in the olive oil. Transfer to a roasting pan and roast for 20–25 minutes, turning halfway through the cooking time.

Meanwhile, make the sauce. Heat the oil in a saucepan and sauté the onion, until soft but not browned. Next, add the garlic and cook for 1 minute. Add the cherry tomatoes and red bell pepper and continue to cook for 3–4 minutes, then add the diced tomatoes, 7-spice, and 1 cup (8 fl oz/250 ml) water. Cook over simmering heat for 20 minutes, stirring occasionally.

Once the eggplant and okra are nicely roasted, remove from the oven and add to the sauce. Add a little more water to the sauce, if necessary, and continue to cook for another 10 minutes. Season to taste with salt and pepper and scatter over the chopped parsley. Serve warm.

See pages 164–165 for photo

FOR THE DOUGH

3 ⅓ cups (15 oz/ 420 g) whole wheat bread (strong wholemeal) flour, plus extra for dusting

2 ½ teaspoons active dry (fast-action)

1 teaspoon salt

3 tablespoons olive oil, plus extra for greasing

milk, for brushing

FOR THE FILLING

4 zucchini (courgettes), trimmed

1 tablespoon olive oil

1 onion, finely chopped

2 garlic cloves, crushed

1 teaspoon Lebanese 7-Spice Seasoning (page 26)

½ teaspoon ground cumin

1 tablespoon sumac

salt and pepper

Zucchini turnovers

This is another classic Lebanese recipe that I love to snack on when I am feeling peckish. I freeze these turnovers (pasties) when I've made a batch and just microwave them for a couple of minutes when I'm ready to serve. They are good for when unexpected guests turn up.

Preparation time: 45 minutes + 1 hour rising
Cooking time: 15 minutes
Makes: 16

For the dough, sift the flour into a bowl. Make a well in the middle and add the yeast to one side and the salt to the other. Pour in the olive oil, then gradually add 1 cup (8 fl oz/250 ml) lukewarm water and mix with a knife to form a dough.

Knead for a few minutes on a floured work surface until you have a smooth dough. Put into a lightly oiled bowl, cover with a dish towel, and let rise in a warm place for about 1 hour.

Meanwhile, make the filling. Grate the zucchini (courgettes), then pat and squeeze dry with paper towels. Set aside in a bowl.

Heat the oil in a skillet or frying pan and sauté the onion until soft but not browned. Add the garlic and spices and cook for 1 minute. Add the onion mixture to the bowl of zucchini and lightly mix together. Season.

Preheat the oven to 400°F/200°C/Gas Mark 6 and line 2 baking sheets with parchment (baking) paper.

Return to the dough and punch down (knock back) for a few minutes on a lightly floured work surface. Divide evenly into 16 balls the size of golf balls. Roll each ball out into a 5-inch/ 13-cm circle and place about 2 heaping tablespoons of filling in each turnover (pasty). Brush the edge of the dough with a little water and then bring the dough up to form a triangle/pyramid shape. Press the edges of the dough together with your fingers to seal.

Place the turnovers on the prepared baking sheets and brush each one with a little milk. Bake for 15 minutes, or until golden.

Ⓥ Substitute the milk with a plant-base milk of your choice.

Ⓖ For the dough, replace the flour with 3 cups (1 lb/450 g) gluten-free whole grain flour blend. Sift the flour into a bowl. Make a well in the middle and add the yeast to one side and 1 teaspoon superfine (caster) sugar and salt to the other. Pour 1 cup (8 fl oz/ 250 ml) lukewarm water into a bowl and add the oil, an egg, and 1 teaspoon white wine vinegar. Whisk together well, then pour slowly into the flour, mixing until a dough forms. Knead on a floured work surface until you have a smooth dough. Put into a lightly oiled bowl, cover with a dish towel, and let rise in a warm place for about 1 hour.

See pages 164–165 for photo

Ⓥ Ⓖ

½ cup (3 ½ oz/100 g) long-grain brown rice

3 eggplants (aubergines), cut into ¾-inch/2-cm cubes

2 tablespoons extra-virgin olive oil

2 onions, finely sliced

4 garlic cloves, finely sliced

2 cups (11 oz/300 g) ripe cherry tomatoes, halved

1 teaspoon ground cumin

1 teaspoon pepper

1 small bunch parsley, leaves chopped

salt

Eggplant with tomatoes and rice

A very simple and warming dish with a sweet flavor from the tomatoes that is offset by warm, aromatic cumin spice. This dish can be served hot, but is even better the day after cooking when it is often served at room temperature.

Preparation time: 25 minutes
Cooking time: 45 minutes
Serves: 4

Bring 1 cup (8 fl oz/250 ml) salted water to a boil and add the rice. Cover and return to a boil. Reduce to a medium heat, simmering for about 30 minutes, or until the rice is tender but retains a little bite. Set aside.

Preheat the oven to 400°F/200°C/Gas Mark 6.

Put the eggplant (aubergine) cubes into a large bowl. Sprinkle with a couple of pinches of salt and add the olive oil. Turn the eggplant around in the oil, then transfer to a baking sheet. Bake for about 20 minutes, or until starting to blacken around the edges. Remove from the oven and set aside.

While the eggplant is baking, heat a little more oil in a skillet or frying pan. Add the onion and garlic and sauté over medium heat for a few minutes, until softened. Add the tomatoes, cumin, and pepper and season with salt. Stir well, then cook for about 15 minutes, until the tomatoes have reduced and the sauce has begun to thicken.

Add the eggplant to the sauce, then stir in the cooked rice. Sprinkle with parsley and serve. Alternatively, let cool and serve the next day either hot or at room temperature.

1 green or white
cabbage, leaves
separated

⅔ cup (4 oz/120 g)
green lentils, rinsed

1 cup (8 fl oz/250 ml)
vegetable broth (stock),
plus a little extra

1 onion, finely chopped

handful chopped
parsley leaves

4 tomatoes, chopped

2 cloves garlic, finely
chopped

juice of 1 lemon

2 tablespoons olive oil

1 teaspoon Lebanese
7-Spice Seasoning
(page 26)

salt and pepper

FOR THE SAUCE

1 tablespoon olive oil

1 onion, finely chopped

3 garlic cloves, finely
chopped

2 tomatoes, finely
chopped

1 ½ teaspoons Tomato
Paste (Puree) (page 27)

⅔ cup (5 oz/150 g)
tomato puree (passata)

1 teaspoon Lebanese
7-Spice Seasoning
(page 26)

salt and pepper

Stuffed cabbage leaves baked in tomato sauce

Herbed lentils are wrapped in cabbage leaves and served with a wonderfully savory sauce. Every Lebanese housewife (and some house husbands) has her own version of this recipe, but this is the one I make time and time again.

Preparation time: 20 minutes
Cooking time: 45 minutes
Serves: 4

Preheat the oven to 400°F/200°C/Gas Mark 6.

Blanch the cabbage leaves in a large saucepan of boiling water for 4 minutes, then drain and rinse under cold water. Set aside.

Add the lentils and vegetable broth (stock) to a saucepan, bring to a boil, then simmer, covered, for 10 minutes, or until cooked through. Add more broth (stock), if necessary. Drain well. Transfer to a bowl and add all the remaining ingredients and mix together. Season with plenty of salt and pepper and set aside.

For the sauce, heat the oil in a large skillet or frying pan over medium heat, then add the onion and garlic and cook until soft but not browned. Add the chopped tomatoes and cook for 2–3 minutes, then add the tomato paste (puree), tomato puree (passata), and 7-spice. Season well and set aside.

Spread out the cabbage leaves on a clean work surface and divide the filling among them. Roll up carefully, tucking in the sides. Gently squeeze the packages to remove any excess liquid and then put them into a deep baking dish and season with salt and pepper.

Pour the sauce over the stuffed cabbage leaves and bake for 30 minutes. Let cool slightly before serving.

2 large eggplants
(aubergines)

4 tablespoons gluten-
free flour

2 teaspoons Lebanese
7-Spice Seasoning
(page 26)

2 tablespoons extra-
virgin olive oil

2 (14-oz/400-g) cans
chickpeas, drained

salt and pepper

FOR THE TOMATO SAUCE

2 tablespoons olive oil

1 onion, finely chopped

4 cloves garlic, finely
chopped

1 teaspoon ground
cumin

1 bay leaf

6 large tomatoes, finely
chopped

7 sun-dried tomatoes,
preserved in oil

2 tablespoons Tomato
Paste (Puree) (page 27)

1 (14 -oz/400-g) can
diced or chopped
tomatoes

1 teaspoon unsweetened
pomegranate molasses

juice of ½ a lemon

salt and pepper

Lebanese vegan moussaka

Every country and every region has their own version of this much-loved dish. This wholesome casserole (called *maghmour*) is a traditional Lebanese way of using simply eggplant, tomato sauce, and chickpeas.

Preparation time: 40 minutes
Cooking time: 50 minutes
Serves: 4

Preheat the oven to 400°F/200°C/Gas Mark 6.

Slice the eggplants (aubergines) into ½-inch/1-cm disks. Mix the flour, spices, and a pinch of salt and pepper on a large plate. Dab each side of the eggplant disks in the flour and spice mix so they are lightly coated. Lay them on a lined baking sheet, drizzle over the olive oil, and bake in the oven for about 10 minutes. Turn, then bake for another 10 minutes, or until crisp. Remove and cool.

In the meantime, make the tomato sauce. Heat the oil in a large skillet or frying pan over medium heat and sauté the onion for 2 minutes. Add the garlic and cook for 1 minute, then add the cumin and bay leaf and cook for another 1–2 minutes. Add the fresh chopped tomatoes, stir, and cook for 3 minutes. Add the sun-dried tomatoes, tomato paste (puree), can of diced tomatoes, one-quarter of the can filled with water, pomegranate molasses, and lemon juice and cook for another 20–30 minutes, stirring occasionally until you have a thick, rich, reduced sauce. Season with salt and pepper. Turn off the heat and set aside. Remove the bay leaf.

Layer the eggplant disks, tomato sauce, and chickpeas in a deep baking pan and repeat until you have used all of your ingredients (3-4 layers, ideally finished with layer of tomato sauce). Bake in the oven for 40 minutes. Set aside to cool.

This really is a dish best served at room temperature when all the flavors are at their best.

4 sweet potatoes, peeled and cut into wedges

1–2 tablespoons olive oil

1 teaspoon cumin seeds

½ cup (3 ½ oz/100 g) long-grain brown rice, washed

1 teaspoon ground cumin

2 large handfuls dried cranberries

1 handful fresh pomegranate seeds (optional)

4 scallions (spring onions), sliced

handful basil leaves

salt and pepper

FOR THE DRESSING

juice of 1 lemon

4 tablespoons olive oil

1 teaspoon Lebanese 7-Spice Seasoning (page 26)

salt and pepper

Roasted sweet potato and cranberry spicy rice

Lemon juice, 7-spice, and good olive oil make a zesty dressing for this sweet potato dish. The dried cranberries and pomegranate seeds add freshness too, lifting the ingredients to more than the sum of their parts.

Preparation time: 15 minutes
Cooking time: 20 minutes
Serves: 4

Preheat the oven to 375°F/190°C/Gas Mark 5.

Put the sweet potato wedges into a large bowl and toss with the olive oil, cumin seeds, salt, and pepper. Spread them out to a baking sheet and roast for 20–25 minutes, or until soft and slightly charred on the edges.

Meanwhile, bring 1 cup (9 fl oz/250 ml) salted water to boil and add the rice and cumin. Cover and return to a boil. Reduce to a medium heat and let simmer for about 30 minutes, or until the rice is tender but retains a little bite. Add more water if necessary.

Mix together the ingredients for the dressing.

Toss the hot rice well with the dressing, cranberries, and pomegranate seeds, if using. Stir in the roasted sweet potatoes gently to avoid breaking them up too much. Top with the scallions (spring onions) and basil and season.

12 baby eggplants
(aubergines)

1 small potato, peeled
and cut into ¾-inch/
2-cm cubes

FOR THE FILLING

⅓ cup (2 ½ oz/75 g)
long-grain rice

1 tomato, coarsely
chopped

1 onion, finely chopped

handful chopped mint
leaves

handful chopped
parsley leaves

1 teaspoon Lebanese
7-Spice Seasoning
(page 26)

½ teaspoon ground
cumin

salt and pepper

**FOR THE
TOMATO SAUCE**

1 ½ teaspoons olive oil

1 small onion, chopped

½ garlic clove, crushed

¾ cup (7 oz/200 g)
canned diced or
chopped tomatoes

3 tablespoons Tomato
Puree (Paste)
(page 27)

½ cinnamon stick

salt and pepper

Stuffed baby eggplants

**Stuffed vegetables are at the heart of every mezze spread
I prepare. These baby eggplants (aubergines) are filled with
seasoned rice and then cooked in a cinnamon-tomato sauce.
They are a delicious example of Lebanese flavor combinations.**

Preparation time: 20 minutes
Cooking time: 50–60 minutes
Serves: 4

For the filling, soak the rice in cold water for 5 minutes and then
drain. Mix with the tomato, onion, herbs, and spices and season
with salt and pepper.

Cut an incision along the lengths of the eggplants (aubergines),
core out the flesh, and discard. If you are using particularly
narrow eggplants, using an apple corer may be helpful here. Stuff
the eggplant with the filling and then plug the end with a cube
of potato to stop the filling from falling out. Set aside.

To make the sauce, heat the oil in a large saucepan and sauté
the onion until slightly golden. Add the garlic and cook for
another minute. Add the diced tomatoes, tomato puree (paste),
cinnamon stick, and 4 ¼ cups (34 fl oz/1 liter) of boiling water.
Season with salt and pepper and bring to a boil. Carefully add the
eggplants to the pan and cook for 45–60 minutes over simmering
heat.

Remove and discard the cinnamon stick. Transfer the
eggplants to a bowl, and serve with the sauce.

Ⓥ Ⓖ

1 cauliflower, broken into florets

1 (14-oz/400-g) can chickpeas, drained and rinsed

5 tablespoons extra-virgin olive oil

1 onion, finely chopped

4 garlic cloves, finely chopped

1 teaspoon ground cumin

1 teaspoon chili flakes

1 ½ teaspoons ground coriander

1 ½ teaspoons garam masala

3 tablespoons Tahini (page 24)

5 teaspoons chickpea (gram) flour, plus extra for dusting

juice of ½ lemon

sea salt and pepper

8 buns, to serve (optional)

1 quantity Fennel and Celery Root Slaw with Sumac (page 131), to serve (optional)

Chickpea and cauliflower patties

These fritters are the ultimate vegan slider. When combined with chickpeas and spices, you get a wonderfully creamy texture inside a crisp outer coating. They are perfect served as burgers in a bun, alongside a refreshing fennel and celery root slaw.

Preparation time: 25 minutes
Cooking time: 7 minutes per fritter
Makes: 8 fritters or 12 smaller sliders

Cook the cauliflower florets in boiling salted water for around 7 minutes. Add the chickpeas and cook for another 7 minutes, or until both are tender. Drain and set aside to cool.

Heat 2 tablespoons of the oil in a skillet or frying pan and sauté the onions and garlic until soft but not browned. Add all of the spices and cook for another 2 minutes. Set aside to cool slightly.

Next, combine the cauliflower, chickpeas, and tahini in a bowl and mash. You can use a fork or pulse them gently in a food processor, but be careful to keep some chunkiness to the consistency. Stir through the chickpea (gram) flour and lemon juice and season with sea salt and pepper.

With cold hands, divide the mixture into 8 patties or 12 smaller sliders. If the patties are still a little wet, dust each side with a little extra chickpea flour.

Heat 1 tablespoon of olive oil in a large skillet and, when it is sizzling hot, add a couple of fritters with a slotted spatula (fish slice). Turn after a couple of minutes and cook the other side. Both sides should be golden and slightly crisp.

Repeat with the remaining fritters and, as they are cooked, drain briefly on paper towels before serving. Serve as is or with buns and slaw, if desired.

2 sweet potatoes, peeled
and chopped into
2-inch/5-cm chunks

2 zucchini (courgettes),
chopped into
1-inch/2.5-cm pieces

4 tablespoons olive oil

2 eggplants (aubergines),
chopped into
1–2-inch/2.5–5-cm
chunks

1 red bell pepper, seeded
and chopped into
1 ½-inch/4-cm chunks

2 onions, finely chopped

7 garlic cloves,
finely chopped

1 teaspoon Lebanese
7-Spice Seasoning
(page 26)

1 teaspoon ground
cumin

1 sprig thyme or
rosemary

6 tomatoes, coarsely
chopped

1 (14-oz/400-g) can
chickpeas, drained

scant ½ cup (3 ½ fl oz/
100 ml) vegetable broth
(stock)

1 tablespoon balsamic
vinegar

sea salt and pepper

brown rice, to serve
(optional)

Msa'aa

**I'd describe this dish as a kind of Lebanese ratatouille.
It is warm and sustaining, and one that people often request
when they're coming to dinner. Traditionally, it is served
slightly cooled, and is sublime when served over hot rice.**

Preparation time: 15 minutes
Cooking time: 1 hour–1 hour 30 minutes
Serves: 4

Preheat the oven to 400°F/200°C/Gas Mark 6.

Arrange the sweet potato and zucchini (courgette) chunks in
a large roasting pan with 2 tablespoons olive oil and season with
sea salt and pepper. Toss well, then roast for 10 minutes.

Add the eggplant (aubergine) and bell pepper to the pan and
roast, stirring occasionally, for another 15 minutes.

Heat the remaining 2 tablespoons olive oil in a skillet or frying
pan over medium heat, add the onions and garlic, and gently cook
for 5 minutes, or until softened. Add the spices and the thyme
or rosemary and cook for another minute. Add the tomatoes,
chickpeas, vegetable broth (stock), and balsamic vinegar and cook
for 10 minutes.

Take the pan of roasted vegetables out of the oven and add the
sauce from the pan. Stir to combine in the roasting pan.

Wrap the top of the pan in aluminum foil (be sure to wear oven
mitts [gloves], because the pan will be hot). Return to the oven
and roast for another 20 minutes, stirring occasionally to let the
vegetables to soak up the sauce.

Remove the foil, stir, and return to the oven to cook for
another 20 minutes.

Remove from the oven, stir again, and let cool for a few minutes.
Remove the thyme or rosemary sprig and serve piled on top of
hot brown rice, if desired.

V G

40 large fresh grape
leaves

2 tablespoons olive oil

salt and pepper

FOR THE STUFFING

¼ cup (2 oz/50 g) green
lentils, rinsed

1 cup (7 oz/200 g) long-
grain rice, washed

1 onion, finely chopped

2 tomatoes, chopped

small handful mint
leaves, finely chopped

small handful parsley
leaves, finely chopped

1 teaspoon Lebanese
7-Spice Seasoning
(page 26)

salt and pepper

Stuffed grape leaves with lentils and rice

Château Musar, the Lebanese wine, is famed the world over but as well as our grapes, we always make the most of our grape leaves. I look forward to summer, when I know there will be plenty in my garden in South London and I can make these every week.

Preparation time: 30 minutes
Cooking time: 30 minutes
Serves: 6 (makes 20)

Bring a large pan of salted water to a boil and blanch the vine leaves for a few seconds. Remove from the pan and let cool on a wire rack.

Take 10 of the grape leaves and lay them over the bottom of a skillet or frying pan, making sure it is completely covered.

To make the stuffing, combine all the stuffing ingredients into a bowl. Season with salt and pepper and mix everything together.

Spread a few of the remaining grape leaves out on a work surface. Take a spoonful of the filling and place across the stalk end of the leaf. Carefully roll into a cigar shape, tucking in the sides. Set aside while you continue making the rest.

Put the 30 stuffed vine leaves in the pan, drizzle with olive oil, and season with salt and pepper. Set a plate slightly smaller than the pan on top of the grape leaves, then pour in enough boiling water to cover both the grape leaves and the plate (the plate keeps them submerged). Cover the pan and cook for 50–60 minutes. Wearing oven mitts (gloves), remove the hot plate.

Transfer the grape leaves to a bowl and serve hot or cold.

3 sweet potatoes, peeled and chopped into coarse chunks

6 tablespoons olive oil

1 onion, finely chopped

6 garlic cloves, finely chopped

1 teaspoon ground cumin

½ teaspoon chili powder

1 (14-oz/400-g) can lentils, drained

2 large handfuls sun-dried tomatoes in oil, coarsely chopped

1 small bunch scallions (spring onions), thinly sliced

½ bunch chopped parsley, leaves finely chopped

salt and pepper

Sweet potato patties

Sweet potatoes, sun-dried tomatoes, and lentils make delicious crisp patties. If I'm making them for a main meal, I shape them into burgers, but if serving with mezze, I make them falafel-size, perfect for dipping into Hummus (page 107) or Baba Ganoush (page 88).

Preparation time: 25 minutes
Cooking time: 20 minutes roasting + 5 minutes to cook each patty
Serves: 4

Preheat the oven to 400°F/200°C/Gas Mark 6.

Toss the sweet potato chunks with 2 tablespoons olive oil, salt, and pepper, then transfer to a baking sheet. Roast for 20 minutes, or until soft inside and turning golden brown.

In the meantime, heat 1 tablespoon of the oil in a skillet or frying pan and gently sauté the onions and garlic with the spices. When they are soft, set aside to cool.

In a mixing bowl, combine the lentils, sun-dried tomatoes, scallions (spring onions), and parsley. Add the roasted sweet potatoes and the onion mixture and mash it all together with a fork, until you have a smooth mashed potato consistency studded with chunks of scallions and sweet potato. Season well with salt and pepper.

With cold hands, shape the mixture into patties or smaller falafel sizes.

Heat the remaining 3 tablespoons of olive oil in a large skillet over medium heat. Add 2 or 3 patties and cook for a few minutes. Carefully turn and cook the other side. Both sides should be golden and slightly crisp.

Repeat with the remaining patties and, as they are cooked, drain briefly on paper towels before serving.

Legumes and Grains

3 tablespoons olive oil,
plus extra to serve

1 ¼ cups (9 oz/ 250 g)
green split peas

4 new potatoes, peeled

1 onion, diced

6 garlic cloves, finely
chopped

2 teaspoons ground
cumin

½ teaspoon pepper, plus
extra to season

1 teaspoon cayenne
pepper

3 cups (25 fl oz/750 ml)
vegetable broth (stock)

3 celery stalks, diced

3 tablespoons chopped
parsley

juice of 1 lemon

Za'atar (page 27), to serve

salt

Green split pea soup

Thicker than many of the split pea soups I have been served in England, this one is wonderfully savory and warming, with plenty of garlic.

Preparation time: 30 minutes
Cooking time: 1 hour
Serves: 4

Preheat the oven to 400°F/200°C/Gas Mark 6. Drizzle 2 tablespoons of the olive oil into a roasting pan and put into the oven to preheat.

Put the split peas into a large saucepan, cover with water, bring to a boil, and cook over medium heat for 15 minutes. Drain and set aside.

Put the potatoes into another saucepan, cover with cold water, and season well. Bring to a boil and cook for 7 minutes. Drain and shake to fluff up.

Heat the remaining oil in a large pot and sauté the onion and garlic for 5 minutes. Add the cumin, pepper, and cayenne pepper, and cook until the onions are soft and slightly browned. Add the potatoes, split peas, broth (stock), celery, and parsley. Return to a boil and simmer until the potatoes and split peas are cooked through.

Use an immersion (stick) blender to puree until smooth, then return to the heat and add the lemon juice and plenty of seasoning. Top up with boiling water to achieve the desired consistency and adjust seasoning to taste.

To serve, pour into bowls, drizzle with olive oil, and finish with a sprinkle of za'atar.

Note: A more traditional variation of this dish is to include roasted potatoes, which gives the soup a nice texture. Add another 4 new potatoes to the recipe and boil them in the pan as instructed. Once drained, coat the 4 potatoes in 3 tablespoons of Za'atar (page 27) and roast in a preheated oven at 400°F/200°C/Gas Mark 6 for 30 minutes, or until golden. To serve, garnish the soup with the potatoes, olive oil, and za'atar.

generous ⅓ cup (2 ½ oz/
75 g) quinoa, rinsed

12 cherry tomatoes,
halved

1 green bell pepper,
seeded and diced

1 cucumber, finely
chopped

1 bunch scallions
(spring onions), finely
sliced

⅔ cup (3 ½ oz/100 g)
cashew nuts, finely
chopped

1 large bunch parsley,
leaves finely chopped

½ bunch mint, leaves
finely chopped

salt and pepper

lemon wedges, to serve
(optional)

FOR THE DRESSING

4 tablespoons extra-
virgin olive oil

juice of 1 lemon

½ teaspoon ground
cumin

½ teaspoon Lebanese
7-Spice Seasoning
(page 26)

salt and pepper

Quinoa tabbouleh

**I love to make tabbouleh in the spring and summer—
The beautiful freshness of the herbs goes well with the
warmer months of the year. Here, I have replaced the
traditional bulgur wheat with quinoa for a different texture,
with the added bonus of making the salad gluten-free.
Cashew nuts add another layer of satisfying crunch, too.**

Preparation time: 15 minutes
Cooking time: 15 minutes
Serves: 4–6

In a saucepan over medium-high heat, bring ⅔ cup (5 fl oz/
150 ml) water to a boil, then add the quinoa. Bring back to a boil
and cook for about 12 minutes, or until tender with a little bite.
Drain, rinse, and squeeze out any excess water. Fluff with a fork
and set aside to cool.

Put the tomato halves into a strainer (sieve) to drain off excess
juices.

Make a dressing in the bottom of a salad bowl. Combine all
the ingredients, then season and mix well.

Add all the remaining ingredients and the cool quinoa to the
bowl and toss to combine. Serve with lemon wedges, if using.

2 cups (14 oz/400 g)
dried pinto beans

1 tablespoon olive oil

2 onions, chopped

1 head garlic, cloves
peeled and chopped

1 tablespoon Za'atar
(page 27)

2 teaspoons Lebanese
7-spice Seasoning
(page 26)

½ teaspoon cayenne
pepper

½ teaspoon ground
cinnamon

2 (14-oz/400-g) cans
diced or chopped
tomatoes

2 tablespoons Tomato
Paste (Puree) (page 27)

small bunch fresh
parsley, finely chopped

2 tablespoons date
molasses or honey

2 tablespoons apple
cider vinegar

salt and pepper

toasted gluten-free
bread, to serve

Pinto beans on toast

When I first came to England, I couldn't believe how many people liked to eat beans on toast—it seemed like the national dish. This is a Middle Eastern take on the staple, with date molasses for depth, and plenty of lively spices to make a warming dinner.

Preparation time: 10 minutes + overnight soaking time
Cooking time: 55 minutes
Serves: 4

Soak the dried beans overnight in plenty of cold water.

Drain the beans, put them into a saucepan, and cover with boiling water. Cook for 30 minutes or until the beans are tender (it will depend how old they are), then drain and set aside.

Meanwhile, heat the oil in a skillet or frying pan and sauté the onions and garlic for 3 minutes, or until slightly golden. Once the onions begin to soften, add the spices and season well. Cook for another 5 minutes, stirring occasionally.

Add the diced tomatoes, tomato paste (puree), parsley, molasses, and vinegar. Stir, then simmer for 20 minutes, letting the sauce reduce.

Add the pinto beans to the pan and cook for another 5 minutes, until they combine well with the sauce. Season with salt and pepper and serve piled on toasted gluten-free bread.

V G

¾ cup (5 oz/150 g) red
quinoa, rinsed

¼ red cabbage, finely
shredded

1 fennel bulb, thinly
sliced

4 scallions (spring
onions), chopped

4 tablespoons extra-
virgin olive oil

juice of 1 ½ lemons

1 tablespoon sumac

1 bunch parsley, leaves
chopped

2 tablespoons chopped
walnuts

salt and pepper

Red quinoa with lemon, cabbage, and sumac

Zesty lemon and tangy sumac elevate this fresh, vibrant salad. I like to use red quinoa here, not only because it tastes subtly different to the standard kind, but because of its pretty color.

Preparation time: 10 minutes
Cooking time: 10 minutes
Serves: 4

In a large saucepan over medium-high heat, bring 1 ¼ cups (10 fl oz/300 ml) water to a boil and add the quinoa. Bring back to a boil and cook for about 12 minutes, or until tender with a little bite. Drain, rinse, and squeeze out any excess water, then fluff with a fork and set aside to cool.

Combine the shredded cabbage, fennel, and scallions (spring onions) in a large bowl. Add the cooked quinoa and toss all the ingredients together.

Mix the olive oil with the lemon juice and sumac. Season well with salt and pepper, then pour the dressing over the salad and mix well to combine. Serve with the chopped parsley and walnuts sprinkled on top.

⅔ cup (4 oz/120 g)
coarse bulgur wheat

2 tablespoons olive oil

2 onions, finely chopped

2 garlic cloves, finely
chopped

1 lb 2 oz/500 g cavolo
nero, finely shredded

1 teaspoon ground
cumin

juice of 1 lemon

salt and pepper

Cavolo nero and bulgur wheat

Making bulgur is a communal activity that brings Lebanese families and villages together at the end of the summer. After the harvest, we like to feast on special seasonal bulgur dishes. Coarse bulgur is traditionally used in dishes such as this one because the texture works well with sturdy vegetables, such as cavolo nero (which is also known as black kale or Tuscan kale). Fine bulgur works too—check the package as cooking times vary depending on the grade you use.

Preparation time: 10 minutes + 30 minutes soaking time
Cooking time: 5–10 minutes
Serves: 3–4

Soak the bulgur wheat in boiling water for 30 minutes, or as directed on the package. Drain well and set aside.

Heat the olive oil in a skillet or frying pan over medium heat. Add the onion and garlic and sauté until soft but not browned.

Add the shredded cavolo nero and cumin to the onion mixture and sauté for another few minutes.

Stir in the drained bulgur wheat, add the lemon juice, and season well before serving.

1 (14-oz/400-g) can
lima (butter) beans,
drained and rinsed

1 (14-oz/400-g) can
black-eyed peas (beans),
drained and rinsed

1 (14-oz/400-g) can
green lentils, drained
and rinsed

4 ¼ cups (34 fl oz/
1 liter) boiling vegetable
broth (stock)

2 tablespoons olive oil

2 onions, finely chopped

3 garlic cloves, finely
chopped

1 teaspoon ground
cumin

1 teaspoon Lebanese
7-Spice Seasoning
(page 26)

1 teaspoon pepper

salt

bread, to serve

Lentil and bean soup

Savory and warming on a winter's day, this lentil and bean soup has a delicious combination of flavors but is simple to prepare, especially if using canned beans and lentils.

Preparation time: 10 minutes
Cooking time: 25 minutes
Serves: 4

Combine the beans, peas, and lentils in a large saucepan and cover with the vegetable broth (stock) and simmer for 10 minutes.

Heat the oil in another large pan. Add the onions and sauté until they start to soften. Add the garlic, cumin, 7-spice, and pepper, and season generously with salt. Cook over low heat, stirring occasionally, until the onions begin to brown.

Add the onions to the ingredients in the other pan and simmer for 30 minutes. If the consistency is too thick, adjust by adding more water. Serve piping hot with bread, which can be topped with za'atar and olive oil.

Note: If using dried legumes, soak them separately overnight in plenty of cold water. You will need 1 ½ cups (8 oz/225 g) each of lima (butter) beans, black-eyed peas (beans), and green lentils. Before starting the recipe, cook as directed on each package until just tender.

¾ cup (5 oz/150 g) dried green lentils, rinsed

5 garlic cloves, 1 whole and 4 crushed

1–2 teaspoons olive oil

2 onions, finely chopped

½ teaspoon Lebanese 7-Spice Seasoning (page 26)

½ teaspoon ground cumin

½ teaspoon ground coriander

½ teaspoon cayenne pepper, plus extra for sprinkling

1 teaspoon Za'atar (page 27)

4 cups (9 oz/250 g) finely chopped cremini (chestnut) mushrooms

2 tablespoons chopped parsley

⅔ cup (3 ½ oz/100 g) cashew nuts, finely chopped

4 tablespoons gluten-free bread crumbs

10 dried apricots, chopped

sunflower oil, for frying

salt and pepper

gluten-free buns, lettuce, and tomatoes, to serve

Lebneh (page 25) and diced cucumber, to serve (optional)

Mushroom, cashew, and apricot burgers

A terrific combination as substantial as any meat burger, these are a hit whenever I serve them. The cashew nuts provide texture and the apricots give a sweet contrast to the savory flavors.

Preparation time: 20 minutes
Cooking time: 45 minutes
Serves: 8

Put the lentils into a saucepan with the whole garlic clove and cover with boiling water. Cook over simmering heat for 30–35 minutes, or until the lentils are soft.

Meanwhile, heat the oil in a skillet or frying pan and sauté the onions until they are soft and slightly colored. Add the crushed garlic and spices and cook for 5 minutes, until the onions begin to brown slightly. Add the mushrooms and parsley and sauté for 10 minutes, then set aside and cool slightly.

In a bowl, mix the cashew nuts with the bread crumbs and season well. Add the cooled onions and mushrooms to the bowl and mix everything together with a wooden spoon. Set aside.

Drain the lentils before transferring them into a large bowl. Mash with a fork until smooth, then add them to the mushroom mixture along with the chopped apricots and season again with salt and pepper.

Mold the mixture into 8 patties with cold hands. If it is crumbly, refrigerate for 30 minutes, until firm.

Heat a few tablespoons of sunflower oil in a large skillet or frying pan over low–medium heat. Add 2 or 3 patties and cook for 3–4 minutes. Turn them carefully and cook the other side. Repeat with the remaining patties and, once they are cooked, drain briefly on paper towels. Carefully transfer onto a plate and serve with gluten-free buns, lettuce, and tomatoes. If desired, serve with lebneh, diced cucumbers, and a sprinkle of cayenne pepper.

¾ cup (7 oz/200 g) drained chickpeas

1 tablespoon olive oil

1 onion, finely chopped

2 garlic cloves, finely chopped

1 red bell pepper, seeded and diced

½ teaspoon chili powder

¼ teaspoon ground turmeric

salt and pepper

Spicy fried chickpeas

A different way to serve chickpeas—it is simple and quick but with really punchy flavors. Removing the skins here does away with any bitterness and allows for spices to really come through.

Preparation time: 10 minutes
Cooking time: 10 minutes
Serves: 4

Roll the chickpeas gently with a rolling pin to release their skins and discard.

Meanwhile, heat the olive oil in a skillet or frying pan and sauté the onion until slightly golden. Add the garlic and red bell pepper and continue to sauté until everything is soft.

Add the chickpeas to the pan and toss well. Add the spices and cook for another few minutes, tossing occasionally, so the chickpeas are completely coated in the spices. Season well and serve hot.

Ⓥ Ⓖ

3 potatoes

scant ⅔ cup (4 ½ oz/ 125 g) red quinoa

1 onion, grated

1 (14-oz/400-g) can chickpeas, drained and rinsed

2 tablespoons finely chopped mint

¼ cup (½ oz/15 g) finely chopped parsley leaves

2 teaspoons ground cumin

1 teaspoon Lebanese 7-Spice Seasoning (page 26)

olive oil, for brushing

salt and pepper

Garlic-Tahini Dip (page 143), to serve

Vegetarian koftas

Brimming with quinoa and chickpeas, these colorful koftas are crisp on the outside and beautifully soft within. Popular as part of a mezze lunch or great for al fresco dining, these bite-size morsels making a lasting impression.

Preparation time: 30 minutes
Cooking time: 1 hour 30 minutes
Serves: 6

Preheat the oven to 400°F/200°C/Gas Mark 6.

Prick the potatoes with a fork and bake for 1 hour, until tender. Remove from the oven, split open, and let cool slightly.

In a saucepan over medium-high heat, bring 1 cup (8 fl oz/ 250 ml) water to a boil, and add the quinoa. Bring back to a boil and cook for about 12 minutes, or until tender with a little bite. Drain, rinse, and squeeze out any excess water. Set aside to cool.

When the potatoes are cool enough to handle, cut them in half, scoop out the flesh, and put it into a bowl. Mash well, then add the quinoa, onion, chickpeas, herbs, and spices and season with salt and pepper. Mix well until thoroughly combined.

Divide into 12 even portions and shape into fat patties or cylinders. Brush each kofta with a little oil, then arrange on a lightly oiled baking sheet. Bake for 30–45 minutes. Serve with garlic-tahini dip, either drizzled over the top or on the side as a dip.

½ cup (3 ½ oz/100 g) coarse bulgur wheat

4 tablespoons sunflower oil

5 onions, 3 sliced and 2 cut into rings

1 ¼ cups (9 oz/250 g) dried Puy or green lentils, rinsed

½ teaspoon ground cumin

½ teaspoon ground coriander

1 teaspoon Lebanese 7-Spice Seasoning (page 26)

salt and pepper

Lentil and bulgur wheat m'juderah

This winning combination of soft lentils, aromatic spices, and crispy onions is one of Lebanon's staple dishes. It is the first dish I remember cooking as a young girl, and I must have made it hundreds of times, because it is so delicious.

Preparation time: 10 minutes + 30 minute soaking time
Cooking time: 40–45 minutes
Serves: 4

First, soak the bulgur wheat in boiling water for 30 minutes, then drain and squeeze out any excess water.

Heat 1 ½ tablespoons sunflower oil in a large skillet or frying pan over medium heat. Add the sliced onions and sauté for about 20 minutes, until soft and golden.

Add the lentils and the spices to the onions, then saute for another minute. Cover with 2 ½ cups (1 pint/600 ml) of boiling water, and cook until the lentils are tender (adding more water, if necessary).

Add the bulgur wheat to the pan and stir to combine. Season well with salt and pepper, then set aside and keep warm.

Heat 2 ½ tablespoons sunflower oil in a large skillet or frying pan over medium heat. Add the onion rings and sauté until crispy and caramelized. Drain on paper towels.

Serve the m'juderah with the crispy onion rings sprinkled on top.

1. Rishta 2. Quinoa and kale 3. Fava beans and rice 4. Mung and green bean salad with toasted pumpkin seeds

5. Chickpea and rice m'juderah

4 ¼ cups (34 fl oz/
1 liter) vegetable broth
(stock)

1 cup (7 oz/200 g) green
lentils, rinsed

¾ cup (2 ½ oz/75 g)
macaroni

1 teaspoon olive oil, plus
extra for drizzling

1 onion, chopped

3 garlic cloves, chopped

3 cups (5 oz/150 g)
shredded spinach leaves

handful chopped
parsley

juice of ½ lemon

salt and pepper

Rishta

This dish, traditionally made with lentils and dough, is one that my grandmother often made when we were children. It's a hearty dish, and it was one of the cheapest she could make that would fill us all up and keep us happy. Some versions of the dish use noodles, tagliatelle, vermicelli—or, in this instance, macaroni—and it is not uncommon to find it in the form of a soup dish.

Preparation time: 10 minutes
Cooking time: 30 minutes
Serves: 4

Bring the vegetable broth (stock) to a boil in a saucepan, then add the lentils. Cook over simmering heat for about 20 minutes, or until the lentils are tender. (Or cook as directed on the package.)

In another saucepan, cook the macaroni in salted boiling water for 8–10 minutes, until tender. Drain and set aside.

Meanwhile, heat the oil in a skillet or frying pan over medium heat. Add the onions and sauté for about 8 minutes, or until soft and caramelized. Add the garlic and cook for another minute.

When the lentils are cooked, add the drained pasta and onion mixture to the pan. Stir through and then add the spinach and parsley. Cook for a few minutes, until the spinach has wilted slightly. Add the lemon juice and drizzle with olive oil. Finally, season to taste with salt and pepper and serve.

Ⓖ Replace the macaroni with corn macaroni.

See pages 210–211 for photo

1 tablespoon olive oil

1 onion, finely chopped

6 garlic cloves, finely chopped

3 cups (7 oz/200 g) chopped curly kale

⅓ cup (2 ¼ oz/60 g) quinoa

1 teaspoon Lebanese 7-Spice Seasoning (page 26)

salt and pepper

Quinoa and kale

This is a beautiful quinoa dish with aromatic garlic and rich green kale.

Preparation time: 5 minutes
Cooking time: 25 minutes
Serves: 4

Heat the oil in a large skillet or frying pan over medium heat. Add the onion and sauté until soft but not colored. Add the garlic and cook for another minute. Add the curly kale and cook, stirring, until wilted and tender.

Meanwhile, cook the quinoa in boiling water as directed on the package. Drain, rinse, and squeeze out any excess water.

Add the quinoa to the pan of kale, stir in the 7-spice, and season with salt and pepper. Cook for another 5 minutes, then serve.

Ⓥ Ⓖ

1 tablespoon olive oil

1 onion, finely chopped

3 garlic cloves, crushed

1 cup (7 oz/200 g) long-grain brown rice, washed

1 teaspoon Lebanese 7-Spice Seasoning (page 26)

1 teaspoon ground cumin

1 ⅓ cups (7 oz/200 g) fresh or frozen fava (broad) beans

large handful chopped parsley

salt and pepper

Fava beans and rice

This is one of my country's most traditional dishes, and it is one that really allows for the unassuming fava (broad) bean to shine. It might be simple, but it is definitely not plain.

Preparation time: 15 minutes
Cooking time: 20 minutes
Serves: 4

Heat the oil in a large skillet or frying pan over medium heat. Add the onion and sauté until soft and slightly golden. Add the garlic and cook for another minute.

Add the rice to the pan and sauté for another few minutes. Add the spices, then pour in 1 ⅔ cups (14 fl oz/400 ml) boiling water to cover the rice. Bring to a boil and cover, then lower the heat and simmer for 15 minutes, or until the rice is nearly cooked and the water has absorbed.

Meanwhile, put the fava (broad) beans into a saucepan and cover with boiling water. Return to a simmer, cover, and cook for 2–4 minutes, or until tender.

Plunge the beans into cold water, then pop them out of their gray outer skins. Add them to the pan with the rice and stir to combine. Season well with salt and pepper and finish with the chopped parsley.

See pages 210–211 for photo

Ⓥ Ⓖ

⅔ cup (3 ½ oz/100 g)
dried mung beans

1 red onion, sliced

2 tablespoons white
wine vinegar

2 cups (7 oz/200 g)
green beans

⅔ cup (3 ½ oz/100 g)
frozen peas

1 tablespoon olive oil

1 teaspoon cumin seeds

1 teaspoon fennel seeds

juice of ½ lemon

handful chopped parsley

1 tablespoon pumpkin
seeds, toasted

salt and pepper

Mung and green bean salad with toasted pumpkin seeds

Quickly pickled onions and toasted pumpkin seeds lift the humble mung bean in this dish, adding both texture and taste—you'll be wanting more.

Preparation time: 10 minutes + overnight soaking time
Cooking time: 40 minutes
Serves: 4

Soak the mung beans overnight in plenty of cold water.

Put the red onion slices into a bowl and add the vinegar. Set aside.

Drain the mung beans, put them into a saucepan and cover with boiling water. Cook for 30 minutes, or as directed on the package. Drain and set aside.

Boil the green beans in salted boiling water for 2 minutes, then drain and let cool slightly. Do the same with the peas.

Heat the olive oil in a skillet or frying pan over medium heat. Add the green beans and cook for a few minutes, or until nearly tender, then add the peas and cook for another 2 minutes. Transfer to a large bowl and wipe the pan clean.

Return the pan to the heat and lightly toast the cumin and fennel seeds.

Transfer the seeds to the bowl with the green beans and peas. Add the mung beans and the lemon juice and toss well. Season with salt and pepper, toss again, then transfer to a large serving platter. Add the chopped parsley, the drained red onion slices, and the pumpkin seeds, then serve immediately.

See pages 210–211 for photo

6 ½ tablespoons
sunflower oil, for frying

5 onions, 3 sliced and
2 cut into rings

½ cup (3 ½ oz/100 g)
long-grain brown rice,
washed

1 (14-oz/400-g) can
chickpeas, drained and
rinsed

2 teaspoons ground
cumin

salt and pepper

Chickpea and rice m'juderah

There are hundreds of ways to serve this humble dish, and different countries across the Levant all have their own spin on it, but, along with the Lentil and Bulgur M'juderah (page 208), this version is an absolute favorite in our house.

Preparation time: 5 minutes
Cooking time: 50 minutes
Serves: 2

Heat 4 tablespoons of the sunflower oil in a large skillet or frying pan over medium heat. Add the sliced onions and sauté for about 20 minutes, until soft.

Add the rice to the onions, cover with a scant 1 cup (7 fl oz/ 200 ml) of boiling water, cover, and cook until the rice is al dente. Add the chickpeas and 1 teaspoon of the cumin to the pan and cook for another 5 minutes, or until the rice is completely cooked. Season well with salt and pepper, then set aside and keep warm.

Heat 2 ½ tablespoons sunflower oil in a skillet or frying pan over medium heat. Add the onion rings and the remaining cumin and sauté until crispy and caramelized. Drain on paper towels.

Serve the m'juderah with the crispy onion rings sprinkled on top.

See pages 210–211 for photo

1 ½ cups (8 oz/225 g) mograbieh

3 shallots, halved

scant 1 cup (7 fl oz/ 200 ml) vegetable broth (stock)

1 (14-oz/400-g) can chickpeas, drained and rinsed

3 tablespoons olive oil

2 onions, finely chopped

½ teaspoon ground cumin

½ teaspoon Lebanese 7-Spice Seasoning (page 26)

1 cup (5 oz/150 g) pine nuts

Himalayan salt and pepper

FOR THE CILANTRO (CORIANDER) DRESSING

1 large bunch cilantro (coriander), leaves chopped, plus extra to garnish

finely grated zest and juice of 1 lemon

4 tablespoons extra-virgin olive oil

Himalayan salt and pepper

Vegetarian mograbieh

It is often the case in the Middle East that a dish will take the name of its primary ingredient, and so it is with mograbieh, also known as Israeli, pearl, or giant couscous. This is the name of a traditional feasting dish, but also the name of the star of the show—a kind of couscous made from durum wheat semolina.

In this recipe, the texture of the couscous still takes center stage, but I have adapted the dish to be served with a fresh herbed dressing.

Preparation time: 15 minutes
Cooking time: 25 minutes
Serves: 3–4

Combine the mograbieh, shallots, and vegetable stock in a large pan. Bring to a boil, then lower the heat, cover, and simmer for 20–30 minutes until the mograbieh is nearly tender. (Or cook as directed on the package.)

Once cooked, drain, then add the chickpeas and mix together well.

Heat 2 tablespoons of the oil in a frying pan over medium heat. Add the onions and season well. Cook for 3 minutes, stirring occasionally. Add the spices and cook for 8 minutes more, or until the onions begin to brown and caramelize. Remove from the heat and set aside.

To make the dressing, put all of the ingredients in a blender, add ¼ cup (2 fl oz/50 ml) water and process for 15 seconds. Set aside until ready to serve.

Heat the remaining tablespoon of olive oil in a large skillet or frying pan. Add the pine nuts and cook until a light golden color. Add the mograbieh-chickpea mixture to the pan and cook for 2–3 minutes. Serve hot in deep bowls, add the onions, and garnish with cilantro (coriander). Serve the dressing on the side and stir through.

Ⓖ Omit step 1 and replace the couscous with an additional 14-oz/400-g can of chickpeas.

1 cup (9 oz/250 g) red
lentils, rinsed

1 cup (7 oz/200 g) fine
bulgur wheat

1 onion, finely chopped

2 tablespoons olive oil,
plus extra for optional
frying

1 teaspoon ground
cumin

2 tablespoons chopped
parsley, to garnish
(optional)

salt and pepper

Red lentil patties

Nutty, and light, these are a delicious traditional Lenten dish.

Preparation time: 20 minutes + cooling time
Cooking time: 35 minutes + 10–12 minutes optional frying time
Makes: 16 patties

Put the lentils into a saucepan with 4 ¼ cups (34 fl oz/1 liter) water and bring to a boil. Reduce the heat to a gentle simmer and cook for 30 minutes, skimming any foam that rises to the surface. Remove from the heat when the lentils are cooked and if there is any water remaining, drain it away completely.

Soak the bulgur in scant 1 cup (7 fl oz/200 ml) boiling water for 15 minutes.

Meanwhile, heat the oil in a skillet or frying pan and add the onion. Add the cumin and sauté until the onion is softened but not browned. Set aside and let cool.

Combine the lentils and bulgur with the onion and season well. When cool enough to handle, bring the mixture together with your hands.

Divide into 16 even portions and shape into cylinders, like fat link sausages, wetting your hands to prevent them from sticking, if necessary.

Traditionally, these are eaten at this stage, but they are also delicious when fried. Cook over medium heat in a little olive oil for 5–6 minutes, turning regularly.

Serve on a platter garnished with chopped parsley, if using.

1 tablespoon olive oil, plus extra for drizzling

2 onions, chopped

2 carrots, cubed

1 leek, sliced

1 celery stalk, chopped

4 garlic cloves, crushed

2 large potatoes, peeled and cubed

4 ¼ cups (34 fl oz/ 1 liter) vegetable broth (stock)

1 ¼ cups (9 oz/250 g) dried green lentils, rinsed

1 bay leaf

1 teaspoon ground cumin

1 teaspoon Lebanese 7-Spice Seasoning (page 26)

10 cups (11 oz/300 g) baby spinach leaves, washed

juice of 1 lemon

salt and pepper

Lebneh (page 25), to serve (optional)

Green lentil and spinach stew

Historically, we have always relied on legumes (pulses) and grains in the Middle East because they are easy to store through the winter, when fresh vegetables and fruit crops are in scarce supply.

Things are changing now, of course. Every time I return to Lebanon, I am surprised at the variety of ingredients available, even sometimes through the seasons. This sustaining stew, however, is still an old favorite—perfection served with a spoon of lebneh.

Preparation time: 10 minutes
Cooking time: 35 minutes
Serves: 6

Heat the oil in a large saucepan. Add the onions, carrots, leek, and celery and cook until soft, but not browned. Next, add the garlic and cook for 1 minute. Add the cubed potatoes, then pour in the broth (stock) and bring to a boil. Add the green lentils and bay leaf and cook over simmering heat until the potatoes and lentils are tender.

Remove the bay leaf, then add the spices and season well with salt and pepper. Add the spinach and cook until wilted, which will take only a few minutes. Finally, add the lemon juice and stir gently to combine. Serve hot, drizzled generously with olive oil and with a spoon of lebneh, if desired

Ⓥ Ⓖ

FOR THE "MEATBALLS"

½ cup (3 ½ oz/100 g) dried green lentils

5 oz/150 g cremini (chestnut) mushrooms

⅔ cup (2 ¾ oz/70 g) drained sun-dried tomatoes

½ cup (2 ¾ oz/70 g) walnuts

1 teaspoon soy sauce

3 tablespoons olive oil

4 garlic cloves, chopped

1 onion, finely chopped

1 celery stalk, chopped

1 carrot, finely chopped

1 teaspoon Lebanese 7-Spice Seasoning (page 26)

1 teaspoon dried oregano

2 tablespoons Tomato Paste (Puree) (page 27)

parsley leaves, to garnish

salt and pepper

FOR THE SAUCE

extra-virgin olive oil

2 garlic cloves, chopped

1 large onion, finely chopped

½ teaspoon cumin

½ teaspoon coriander

pinch of chili flakes

6 tomatoes, chopped

1 cup (8 fl oz/250 ml) vegetable broth (stock)

1 (14-oz/400-g) can diced tomatoes

1 tablespoon Tomato Paste (Puree) (page 27)

handful basil leaves, torn

Lentil "meatballs"

Lentils lend a substantial texture to these balls, making them every bit as satisfying as their more conventional non-vegetarian counterparts. Generously spiced and served drenched in tomato sauce, they are both slightly unusual and decidedly delicious.

Preparation time: 20 minutes
Cooking time: 20 minutes
Serves: 4

Preheat the oven to 400°F/200°C/Gas Mark 6 and lightly oil a baking sheet.

Rinse the lentils and put them into a saucepan and cover with boiling water. Cook over simmering heat for 30–35 minutes, or until the lentils are soft and the water has been absorbed.

Put the mushrooms, sun-dried tomatoes, walnuts, and soy sauce into a food processor. Add 2 tablespoons olive oil and a pinch of salt and pepper and blend to a paste.

Heat the remaining oil in a skillet or frying pan over medium heat and sauté the garlic for 1 minute. Add the onion, celery, and carrot and sauté until soft but not colored. Add the 7-spice and oregano and season well.

Add the mushroom paste to the skillet or frying pan and cook over low heat for another 2–3 minutes. Add the cooked lentils and cook for another 2 minutes, stirring occasionally. Finally, add the tomato paste (puree) and cook for 1 minute, stirring. Set the mixture aside until it is cool enough to handle.

Shape the mixture into balls the size of golf balls and place on the prepared baking sheet. Bake for 20 minutes, or until golden and slightly crispy.

To make the sauce, heat a tablespoon of olive oil in a saucepan. Add the garlic and sauté for 1 minute without browning. Add the onion, season with a little salt, and sauté until softened. Add the spices and chili flakes and cook for another minute, stirring occasionally.

Stir in the chopped tomatoes and cook for 2 minutes. Add the vegetable broth (stock), the canned tomatoes, and the tomato paste and bring to a boil. Season with a little more salt and pepper and add the basil leaves. Bring to a boil, then reduce the heat and simmer over low heat for about 10 minutes, stirring occasionally, or until the until the liquid has reduced to a thick tomato sauce.

Serve the "meatballs" with plenty of piping hot tomato sauce and a sprinkle of fresh parsley.

½ cup (2 ½ oz/75 g) fine bulgur wheat

2 potatoes, peeled and cut into chunks

⅔ cup (4 ½ oz/125 g) dried green lentils, rinsed

¾ cup (2 ½ oz/75 g) dried bread crumbs

1 small bunch parsley, leaves only

1 small bunch mint, leaves only

1 onion, finely chopped

½ teaspoon Lebanese 7-Spice Seasoning (page 26)

½ teaspoon ground cumin

3 tablespoons olive oil

salt and pepper

Bulgur falafel

This is one of my favorite, family-friendly recipes. They can sandwiched with pita (page 70) and a dip, such as the Fava Bean and Artichoke Dip (page 86) or the Garlic-Tahini Dip (page 143).

Preparation time: 20 minutes
Cooking time: 25 minutes + 6–8 minutes to cook the patties
Makes: 8

Soak the bulgur in ⅓ cup (2 ½ fl oz/75 ml) boiling water for 15 minutes, or as directed on the package. Drain well.

Boil the potatoes in plenty of salted boiling water for 8 minutes, or until tender. Drain and let steam dry, then transfer to a bowl.

Meanwhile, in a separate saucepan, boil the lentils in plenty of unsalted boiling water until tender. Drain well.

In a blender or food processor, combine the potatoes, lentils, bulgur wheat, ½ teaspoon pepper, and all the remaining ingredients except for the oil. Pulse to combine, but do not overprocess: the mixture should be smooth but retain some texture. Season well.

Mold the mixture into 8 equal patties, ½–¾ inch/1–2 cm thick. Flour them to prevent them from sticking, if necessary.

Heat 1 tablespoon of the oil in a large skillet or frying pan over medium heat. Cook the patties in batches for 3–4 minutes on each side, or until golden, crisp, and heated through. Serve warm.

Desserts

(G)

7 tablespoons (3 ½ oz/ 100 g) unsalted butter, plus extra for greasing

4 tablespoons corn (golden) syrup or agave

2 cups (7 oz/200 g) gluten-free oats

⅔ cup (3 ½ oz/100 g) chopped dates

1 sweet, crisp apple, peeled, cored, and grated

1 banana, mashed

⅓ cup (2 oz/50 g) pumpkin seeds

1 teaspoon ground cinnamon

½ teaspoon grated nutmeg

1 teaspoon ground ginger

½ teaspoon Himalayan salt

Spiced date oat bars

These popular afternoon treats are gently spiced with cinnamon and crammed with dates and pumpkin seeds. They are a great snack to pack for long journeys and are popular with all ages.

Preparation time: 10 minutes
Cooking time: 30 minutes
Serves: 12

Preheat the oven to 375°F/190°C/Gas Mark 5. Grease a 6 × 10 inch/ 15 × 25 cm baking pan and line with parchment (baking) paper.

Combine the butter and syrup or agave in a large saucepan and heat gently, stirring occasionally, until the butter has melted. Remove from the heat and add the remaining ingredients. Stir well to combine.

Spoon the mixture into the prepared pan and press in firmly. Bake for 30 minutes, until golden on top.

Remove from the oven and cut into 12 squares. Let cool in the pan to cool and firm up a little before removing.

V Replace the butter with a dairy-free alternative.

Ⓥ Ⓖ

1 orange, peeled and
sliced

1 apple, peeled, cored,
and sliced

1 pear, peeled, cored,
and sliced

2 kiwis, peeled and
sliced

6 strawberries, halved

12 grapes, halved

seeds from
1 pomegranate

FOR THE SYRUP

⅔ cup (4 oz/120 g)
superfine (caster) sugar

1 lemon leaf

handful mint leaves,
chopped, plus extra to
garnish

Fresh fruit salad with mint syrup

This classic fruit salad served with a fresh mint syrup is a light and traditional way to end a traditional Middle Eastern mezze meal.

Preparation time: 20 minutes
Cooking time: 15 minutes
Serves: 4

Combine the fruit in a large bowl and toss together.

For the syrup, put the sugar, lemon leaf, and mint into a saucepan with ½ cup (4 fl oz/120 ml) water. Cook on medium heat and boil, without stirring, for 10–15 minutes, until the syrup has thickened. Remove from the heat and let cool, then pour the syrup over the fruit and mix well. Garnish with mint leaves.

Ⓥ Ⓖ

1 lb 2 oz/500 g
strawberries, hulled

¾ cup (5 oz/150 g)
superfine (caster) sugar

2 teaspoons rosewater

squeeze of lemon juice

chopped pistachios, for
topping

Strawberry-rose sorbet

**Delicate, pretty, and refreshing, this is the queen of sorbets.
Serve by itself in decorative glasses or with Strawberry,
Raspberry, and Honey Compote (page 71).**

Preparation time: 10 minutes + freezing time
Makes: 3 cups (1 lb 5 oz/600 g)

Put the strawberries, sugar, rosewater, and lemon juice into
a blender or processor and process until smooth.

Freeze in an ice cream maker according to the manufacturer's
instructions. Alternatively, put the mixture into a freezer-proof
container and freeze for 1 ½ hours. Break up the ice crystals with
a fork and repeat two times before serving.

Serve with a sprinkling of pistachio nuts.

Ⓖ

⅔ cup (5 fl oz/150 ml)
pomegranate juice

⅔ cup (5 fl oz/150 ml)
plain Greek-style yogurt
or Lebneh (page 25)

1 tablespoon honey

1 vanilla bean

seeds from
1 pomegranate

Pomegranate-yogurt ice pops

A colorful treat that I often made for my grandchildren when they were growing up. The combination of creamy yogurt and sweet/sour pomegranate is wonderful.

Preparation time: 15 minutes + freezing time
Makes: 6 ice pops (ice lollies)

Pour equal amounts of pomegranate juice into ¼ cup (2 fl oz/ 50 ml) ice pop (ice lolly) molds, filling each one halfway. Freeze for 1 hour, or until the juice is beginning to harden but is not completely frozen.

In a bowl, combine the yogurt or lebneh and honey. Split the vanilla bean lengthwise and scrape the seeds into the bowl. Stir to combine.

Remove the molds from the freezer, push in the sticks, and top up with the yogurt mixture. To get a marbled effect, stir the pomegranate and the yogurt together briefly. Finish with a sprinkling of seeds. Return to the freezer for several hours, or until completely frozen.

To remove the ice pops from the molds, dip very briefly in hot water.

Ⓥ For a vegan-friendly option, replace the yogurt with unsweetened soy milk and the honey with agave.

Honeydew-orange flower sorbet

Ⓥ Ⓖ

3 cups (1 lb 2oz/500 g)
diced honeydew melon

4 tablespoons superfine
(caster) sugar

2 teaspoons orange
flower water

When the sun comes out, I want to eat melon. Honeydew and orange flower water are a wonderfully cooling combination in this fresh green sorbet.

Preparation time: 10 minutes + freezing time
Makes: 2 ¾ cups (1 lb 4 oz/560 g)

Process the melon, sugar, and orange flower water in a blender.

Freeze in an ice cream maker according to the manufacturer's instructions. Alternatively, put the mixture into a freezer-proof container and freeze for 1 ½ hours. Break up the ice crystals with a fork and repeat two more times before serving.

4 extra-large (UK large)
egg whites

1 cup (7 oz/200 g)
superfine (caster) sugar

¾ cup (4 oz/100 g)
shelled pistachios,
chopped

⅔ cup (5 fl oz/150 ml)
heavy (double) cream

1 teaspoon rosewater

3 tablespoons
confectioners' (icing)
sugar

salt

Pistachio meringues
with rose cream

Crumbly pistachio and meringue sandwiched together with layers of fragrant rose-scented cream—what's not to like? They bring together two quintessential flavors of the Middle East, and are a perfect summer dessert, especially if you have just eaten a large mezze spread.

Preparation time: 30 minutes
Cooking time: 1 hour–1 hour 30 minutes
Makes: 16 meringues, 8 sandwiched with cream

Preheat the oven to 275°F/140°C/Gas Mark 1 and line two baking sheets with parchment (baking) paper.

Whisk the egg whites with a pinch of salt until stiff peaks form. Add the superfine (caster) sugar, a little at a time, while continuing to whisk. Fold in half of the chopped pistachios with a large metal spoon.

Spoon the meringue onto the prepared baking sheets, dividing evenly to make 16 mounds. Bake for 1 hour, checking and turning the sheets halfway through the cooking time. The meringues are ready when firm. Loosen from the paper and let cool on the baking sheets.

Beat the cream, rosewater, and confectioners' (icing) sugar together until thickened. Sandwich the meringues together with the cream, and sprinkle the extra pistachios around the edge of the meringue.

1 (14-oz/400-g) can chickpeas, drained and rinsed

1 tablespoon mild olive oil

3 teaspoons superfine (caster) sugar

1 teaspoon allspice

Sweet roasted chickpeas

I snacked on sugared chickpeas a lot as child, so this is a nostalgic thing for me. These are an addictive snack, but they also make a delicious and crunchy addition to fresh fruit, yogurt, or ice cream.

Preparation time: 10 minutes
Cooking time: 30 minutes
Serves: 2–4

Preheat the oven to 350°F/180°C/Gas Mark 4.

After rinsing, let the chickpeas drain in the strainer (sieve) for a few minutes, then pour onto a tray covered with paper towels. Gently press more paper towels on top to absorb as much liquid as possible. Remove the skins.

Pour the oil into a shallow, baking pan, together with the chickpeas. Add the sugar and spice and mix with your hands to make sure there is an even coating. Spread the chickpeas into a single layer and roast for 30 minutes, shaking occasionally, until golden brown and crunchy. Let cool before eating.

1 ½ cups (5 oz/150 g)
dry bread crumbs

1 ¼ cups (10 fl oz/
300 ml) soy cream

2 ½ cups (20 fl oz/
600 ml) soy milk

⅔ cup (4 oz/120 g) fine
or coarse semolina

½ cup (3 ½ oz/100 g)
superfine (caster) sugar

1 tablespoon orange
flower water

edible petals, to serve

FOR THE SYRUP

1 cup (7 oz/200 g)
superfine (caster) sugar

2 lemon leaves

juice of 2 lemons

Konafah with lemon syrup

This typical Lebanese dessert is creamy and indulgent. Thought often made with vermicelli, I like to use bread crumbs for a different texture. The orange flower water custard is beautifully offset by golden crumbs.

Preparation time: 20 minutes
Cooking time: 30-40 minutes
Serves: 6-8

Preheat the oven to 400°F/200°C/Gas Mark 6.

Pour half of the bread crumbs into a 9-inch/23-cm square baking dish and toast them in the oven for 10 minutes, or until just brown.

Reduce the oven to 350°F/180°C/Gas Mark 4.

In a saucepan over medium heat, combine the cream, milk, semolina, sugar, and orange flower water, mix well, and cook for 10 minutes or until slightly thickened.

Pour the cream mixture on top of the bread crumbs and top with the rest of bread crumbs. Bake for 15 minutes or until the bread crumbs are golden and the mixture is firm. Sprinkle with edible flowers, if desired.

For the syrup, combine the sugar, lemon leaves, and a scant 1 cup (7 fl oz/200 ml) water in a small saucepan over medium heat, stir, and simmer for 10 minutes, or until it becomes a thick syrup. Remove the leaves, add the lemon juice, and mix well.

Serve slices of the dessert warm with the lemon syrup.

5 Jazz or Royal Gala apples, peeled, cored, and coarsely chopped

¼ cup (2 oz/50 g) firmly packed light (soft) brown sugar

1 cinnamon stick

⅔ cup (3 ½ oz/100 g) chopped, pitted dates

plain (natural) yogurt or Lebneh (page 25), to serve

FOR THE TOPPING

1 ¼ cups (5 ½ oz/150 g) all-purpose (plain) flour

5 tablespoons (2 ½ oz/ 75 g oz) unsalted butter, chilled and diced

⅓ cup (2 ½ oz/75 g) turbinado (demerara) sugar

Spiced apple and date crumble

This popular dessert has a warm caramel flavor from the combination of apples, cinnamon, and dates that will warm any winter night. Topped with my classic crunchy topping, this crumble is hard to resist.

Preparation time: 15 minutes
Cooking time: 50 minutes
Serves: 6

Put the apples into a saucepan with the sugar and cinnamon stick. Stew over medium-low heat for 20 minutes, or until the apples are soft. Remove the cinnamon stick and mash to a puree, then mix in the chopped dates and set aside to cool.

Preheat the oven to 375°F/190°C/Gas Mark 5.

To make the topping, use your fingertips to rub the butter into the flour until you have a coarse mixture that resembles bread crumbs. Add the sugar and mix together.

Spoon the apple-and-date filling into a 9-inch/23-cm pie dish and sprinkle on the topping. Bake for 30 minutes, or until the topping is golden and the apples are bubbling from underneath. Serve warm with creamy yogurt.

Ⅴ Replace the butter with ½ cup (3 ½ oz/100 g) solid virgin coconut oil.

Ⓖ Replace the flour with a gluten-free alternative.

4 ¼ cups (34 fl oz/
1 liter) low-fat (semi-
skimmed) milk

1 egg, lightly beaten

½ cup (3 ½ oz/100 g)
superfine (caster) sugar

1 tablespoon ginger
wine

1 cup (5 ½ oz/150 g)
all-purpose (plain) flour

1 teaspoon vanilla
extract

2 ¼ cups (9 oz/
250 g) graham crackers
(digestive biscuits)

5 tablespoons (2 ½ oz/
65 g) butter, melted

¾ cup (2 oz/50 g) dried
(desiccated) coconut

Coconut and ginger cake

**An indulgent classic dessert with a pleasant kick from
a warming addition of ginger wine.**

Preparation time: 5 minutes + 1 hour 30 minutes setting time
Cooking time: 20 minutes
Makes: 1 (8-inch/20-cm) cake

In a large saucepan, combine the milk, egg, sugar, ginger wine,
flour, and vanilla and mix together. Bring the mixture to a boil,
stirring continuously, then reduce the heat to a simmer and
cook for 10 minutes, or until you have the thickness of custard.
Remove from the heat and let cool slightly.

Line an 8-inch/20-cm loose-bottom cake pan with plastic
wrap (clingfilm).

Process the graham crackers (digestive biscuits) in a food
processor to crumbs. Pour half of the crumbs into a bowl and mix
well with the melted butter. Arrange the mixture in a layer over
the bottom of the lined cake pan. Pour half the custard over
the top and refrigerate for 1 hour to set. Add the remaining half
of the graham cracker crumbs and pour on the remaining custard.
Sprinkle with dried (desiccated) coconut, and refrigerate for
another 30 minutes before serving.

1. Ma'mool cookies 2. Almond pistachio cookies 3. Tahini and pomegranate cookies 4. Anise and sesame cookies

FOR THE DOUGH

1 stick (4 oz/120 g) unsalted butter, melted

1 ⅓ cups (8 oz/225 g) coarse semolina

2 tablespoons sugar

1 teaspoon mahleb

⅔ cup (3 ½ oz/100 g) all-purpose (plain) flour, plus extra for dusting

½ teaspoon baking soda (bicarbonate of soda)

1 tablespoon orange blossom water

confectioners' (icing) sugar, for dusting

FOR THE WALNUT FILLING

½ cup (2 oz/50 g) finely chopped walnuts

½ teaspoon sugar

1 teaspoon orange blossom water

FOR THE PISTACHIO FILLING

⅓ cup (2 oz/50 g) shelled pistachio nuts

½ teaspoon sugar

1 teaspoon orange blossom water

FOR THE DATE FILLING

⅓ cup (2 oz/50 g) pitted chopped dates

½ teaspoon sugar

1 teaspoon allspice

Ma'mool cookies

This is probably my favorite cookie (biscuit) recipe to make, because they taste like nothing else on Earth. I have had my ma'mool molds for many years and the different shape of each one tells you which filling will be inside it. Goodness knows how many cookies have shaped over the years!

Preparation time: 20 minutes + 3 hours/overnight standing time
Cooking time: 20–30 minutes
Makes: 12–18

To make the dough, melt the butter in a large saucepan, then stir in the semolina, sugar, and mahleb. Push the mixture down into the pan, cover, and remove from the heat. Let stand for at least 3 hours, or overnight, at room temperature.

To make the walnut filling, put the ingredients into a blender or food processor and process to fine crumbs. Repeat for the pistachio filling and then the date filling. Keep them separated.

Return the pan of semolina mixture to a low heat for a few minutes to loosen, then remove from the heat and transfer into a bowl. Add the flour, baking soda (bicarbonate of soda), orange blossom water, and 1 tablespoon of water. Knead the mixture in the bowl for 5–10 minutes, until a dough forms. Add another 2–3 tablespoons of water, if required.

Preheat the oven to 325°F/160°C/Gas Mark 3.

To make the ma'mool, take a handful of dough and dust with flour, then flatten into a patty with your hands. Put 1 teaspoon of filling in the center of the patty and then wrap the dough around the filling. Roll in flour, then press into a ma'mool mold. Tap the mold on the work surface to release the cookie and put it onto a baking sheet. If you don't have molds, use an individual gelatin (jelly) mold or cut a decorative shape with a ravioli cutter.

Repeat this filling and shaping until all the dough and filling mixtures have been used. Any leftover filling can be frozen.

Bake for 25–30 minutes, until golden. Remove from the oven and transfer the cookies to a wire rack to cool completely. Dust with confectioners' (icing) sugar. Store in an airtight container.

Ⅴ Replace the butter with a dairy-free alternative.

Ⓖ For the dough: Combine ⅓ cup (2 ¼ oz/60 g) cashew nuts, 1 cup (4 ¾ oz/130 g) finely chopped walnuts, 2 ¾ cups (14 oz/400 g) pitted dates, 4 ½ tablespoons (2 ¼ oz/60 g) unsalted butter, and ⅓ cup (2 ¼ oz/60 g) gluten-free flour in a food processor and process until smooth. Transfer to a bowl and roll into a dough. The dough will cook faster than the traditional version, so check after 15 minutes.

See pages 248–249 for photo

Ⓖ

7 tablespoons (3 ½ oz/ 100 g) unsalted butter

¼ cup (3 ½ oz/100 g) agave syrup

1 cup (3 ½ oz/100 g) almond meal (ground almonds)

few drops of vanilla extract

generous ¾ cup (5 oz/ 140 g) rice flour (ground rice)

1 teaspoon baking soda (bicarbonate of soda)

⅓ cup (2 oz/50 g) shelled pistachios, crushed

Almond pistachio cookies

I pack these with plenty of nuts, which gives them a beautiful crumb. They are particularly lovely when dunked into a glass of almond milk.

Preparation time: 15 minutes
Cooking time: 15–20 minutes
Makes: 20

Preheat the oven to 350°F/180°C/Gas Mark 4 and line a baking sheet with parchment (baking) paper.

Combine the butter and syrup in a bowl and beat until pale and creamy. Add the almond meal (ground almonds) and continue to beat. Next, add the vanilla extract.

Sift in the rice flour (ground rice) and baking soda (bicarbonate of soda) and mix in thoroughly. Finally, add the pistachios and mix again to form a dough.

Flour your hands, make a walnut-size lump of dough, and roll into a ball. Place on the prepared baking sheet and flatten gently with your fingers. Repeat until all the dough is used.

Bake for 15–20 minutes. Remove from the oven and let cool slightly before transferring the cookies to a wire rack to cool completely.

Ⓥ Replace the butter with a dairy-free alternative.

See pages 248–249 for photo

Ingredients

2 ⅓ cups (11 oz/300 g) all-purpose (plain) flour, plus extra for dusting

½ teaspoon baking powder

1 ¼ sticks (5 oz/150 g) unsalted butter, diced

⅔ cup (5 oz/150 g) granulated sugar

1 egg, beaten

1 tablespoon Tahini (page 24)

1 tablespoon rosewater

½ pomegranate, seeds only

2 oz/50 g white chocolate, chopped into small chunks

Tahini and pomegranate cookies

The jewel-like pomegranate seeds stud the dough, making these cookies as pretty as they are delicious. The taste of tahini is delicate and they have a crisp texture. I like to enjoy a couple of them with a nice cup of tea.

Preparation time: 20 minutes
Cooking time: 15–20 minutes
Makes: 20–24

Preheat the oven to 350°F/180°C/Gas Mark 4 and line a baking sheet with parchment (baking) paper.

Sift the flour and baking powder into a large bowl, then add the butter and rub in with your fingertips until the mixture resembles fine bread crumbs. Stir in the sugar.

Gradually stir in the egg, then add the tahini, rosewater, pomegranate seeds, and chocolate and bring the mixture together to form a dough. Add more flour if it is too sticky.

Roll out to ⅛–¼ inch/3–5mm thick and use a 3 ¼-inch/8-cm cutter to stamp out. Re-roll as necessary to cut 20–24 cookies.

Place the cookies on the prepared baking sheet, allowing space between them. You will fill 3 baking sheets, because these are large cookies, so bake in batches.

Bake for 15–20, until golden brown. Let cool for 5 minutes before transferring to a wire rack to cool further.

Ⓖ Replace the flour and baking powder with gluten-free alternatives and bake for 20–25 minutes.

See pages 248–249 for photo

Anise and sesame cookies

This recipe was one my Auntie Hannah made often. They really do melt in the mouth and one is never enough! I use plenty of ground anise seeds, which are offset by the bittersweet flavor of mahleb (see glossary on page 20).

1 ⅓ cups (5 ¾ oz/165 g) all-purpose (plain) flour

2 ¼ teaspoons baking powder

¼ cup (2 oz/50 g) superfine (caster) sugar

¼ cup (1 ¼ oz/35 g) sesame seeds

1 tablespoon ground anise seed

1 teaspoon mahleb

1 heaping tablespoon sunflower oil

2 tablespoons milk, plus extra for glazing

1 egg

Preparation time: 15 minutes
Cooking time: 15 minutes
Makes: 16

Preheat the oven to 350°F/180°C/Gas Mark 4 and line 2 baking sheets with parchment (baking) paper.

Put all the dry ingredients into a large bowl and mix together.

Combine the oil, milk, and egg in a separate bowl and whisk together with a fork.

Make a well in the dry ingredients and pour in the oil mixture. Use a wooden spoon to bring the ingredients together to form a dough.

With slightly damp hands, divide the dough into 16 equal pieces. Roll each piece into a cylinder and bring the ends together, pinching gently to seal. Repeat until all the dough is used, transferring them to the baking sheets as you work. Make sure you allow room between each cookie (biscuit).

Brush with a little milk and bake for 15–20 minutes. Remove from the oven, let cool, and then transfer to a wire rack.

Ⓖ Replace the flour and baking powder with gluten-free alternatives.

See pages 248–249 for photo

3 ⅓ cups (1 lb 2 oz/
500 g) unsalted peanuts
(groundnuts)

1 ¼ cups (7 oz/200 g)
sesame seeds

1 cup (12 oz/340 g)
honey

2 tablespoons superfine
(caster) sugar

1 teaspoon orange
flower water

Sesame seed bars

These bars are a popular snack in Lebanon. I like to make them myself because you can get the quantities of sesame seeds, peanuts (groundnuts), honey, and orange flower water just as you want them. There is also nothing better than freshly toasted sesame seeds. Use a sugar thermometer to get the temperature right, because this is vital to getting the characteristic brittle texture here.

Preparation time: 5 minutes + overnight setting time
Cooking time: 25 minutes
Makes: 20 bars

Preheat the oven to 375°F/190°C/Gas Mark 5 and line an
8 × 12-inch/20 × 30-cm baking pan with parchment (baking) paper. Set aside.

Sprinkle the peanuts (groundnuts) into a clean roasting pan and roast for 15 minutes. Transfer into a large mixing bowl.

Toast the sesame seeds in a dry skillet or frying pan and add to the peanuts.

Put the honey, sugar, and orange flower water into a saucepan and heat to 300°F/150°C. Once it reaches this temperature, pour onto the peanuts and sesame seeds and stir to combine.

Pour the mixture into the prepared pan and press into an even layer. Let set for 4 hours or overnight. Slice into 20 bars.

Pistachio walnut halva

Ⓖ

scant 1 cup (9 oz/250 g)
Tahini (page 24), plus
extra to grease

⅔ cup (2 ¾ oz/80 g)
shelled pistachios

⅔ cup (2 ¾ oz/80 g)
walnuts

generous 1 cup
(9 oz/250 g) honey

1 teaspoon almond
extract or orange flower
water

One of the Middle East's most prized treats, homemade halva is a thing of beauty. I serve mine straight from the refrigerator, alongside bitter Black Coffee (page 43) for a light snack. Use any combination of nuts you want as long as it amounts to 1 ⅓ cups (5 ½ oz/160 g.)

Preparation time: 10 minutes + 24 hours setting time
Cooking time: 15 minutes
Makes: around 25 pieces

Grease an 8-inch/20-cm baking pan with a little tahini.

Heat a dry skillet or frying pan over medium heat and toast the pistachios and walnuts until golden. Remove from the heat and set aside.

Put the honey into a heavy saucepan over medium heat. Boil until it reaches the "soft ball" stage, which is 245°F/118°C on a candy (sugar) thermometer. Take the pan off the heat and let cool slightly before stirring in the nuts, almond extract or orange flower water, and the tahini. Mix thoroughly to combine.

Pour in the mixture and use the back of a spoon to smooth the surface evenly.

Refrigerate for 24 hours before cutting.

6 sheets phyllo (filo) pastry (covered with a damp cloth to prevent them from drying)

unsalted butter, melted, for brushing the phyllo

FOR THE FILLING

¾ cup (3 ½ oz/100 g) shelled pistachios

1 ¼ cups (5 oz/150 g) chopped walnuts

⅓ cup (2 ½ oz/75 g) superfine (caster) sugar

2 tablespoons rosewater

FOR THE SUGAR SYRUP

1 cup (7 oz/200 g) superfine (caster) sugar

1 tablespoon rosewater

1 lemon leaf (optional)

Baklava rolo

Baklava is one of the most famous sweet treats from the Levant and rightly so—it is indulgent, buttery, and delicious when done well. Dessert is about pleasure, and this one will satisfy even the sweetest tooth. A little goes a long way!

Preparation time: 30 minutes
Cooking time: 20 minutes
Makes: 28 pieces

For the filling, put the nuts and sugar into a food processor and process until coarsely ground. Stir in the rosewater, then transfer into a bowl.

To make the sugar syrup, put the sugar into a saucepan, pour in a scant 1 cup (7 fl oz/200 ml) water, and stir over low heat until all the sugar has dissolved. Increase the heat and boil to a syrupy consistency. Remove from the heat, stir in the rosewater, and add the lemon leaf, if using. Let cool completely to allow the flavors to infuse.

Preheat the oven 350°F/180°C/Gas Mark 4 and line 2 baking sheets with parchment (baking) paper.

Take 1 sheet of phyllo (filo) and cut it into 4 smaller pieces, each 8 ½ x 4 inches/22 × 10 cm. Repeat this with the remaining 5 sheets of the phyllo so you have a total of 24 smaller pieces. Cover the pastry with a damp cloth to stop it from drying out.

Lay 2 pieces of phyllo out on a clean, dry work surface, with the longest sides toward you. Lightly brush both sheets with melted butter and lift one sheet on top of the other. Sprinkle on some of the filling to cover the surface completely. Brush 2 more phyllo pieces with butter, lay them on top, and sprinkle with more filling. Repeat with 2 more pieces of phyllo and a final layer of filling.

Next, roll the phyllo up into a fat log, starting from the closest edge to you. Brush all over with a little melted butter. Slice into 7 pieces and lay them on the prepared baking sheet.

Repeat with the remaining phyllo, butter, and filling to achieve a total of 28 small baklava pieces. Arrange on a prepared baking sheet (using 2 if needed) and bake for 20 minutes, or until nice and golden. Let cool completely and then pour on the syrup and let stand until absorbed.

1 ½ sticks (6 oz/170 g) softened butter, plus extra for greasing

5 cardamom pods

4 ripe bananas, mashed

generous ¾ cup (6 oz/170 g) superfine (caster) sugar

3 eggs

1 cup (4 oz/115 g) chopped walnuts

2 ¾ cups (12 oz/350 g) all-purpose (plain) flour

¼ teaspoon baking soda (bicarbonate of soda)

2 ¾ teaspoons baking powder

½ teaspoon salt

confectioners' (icing) sugar, to serve (optional)

Cardamom banana cake

I love the comforting combination of the texture and taste of banana cake. This recipe is fragrant with cardamom, a spice that goes really well with the subtle sweetness of the fruit. Banana cake is popular around the world in many shapes and forms, and the cardamom just gives it our Levantine twist. Use ripe bananas for the best results.

Preparation time: 20 minutes
Cooking time: 35–40 minutes
Serves: 8

Preheat the oven to 350°F/180°C/Gas Mark 4 and grease a nonstick 10-inch/25-cm square cake pan.

Crush the cardamom pods, removing the seeds and discarding the pods. Crush the seeds to release their flavor, add them to the mashed bananas, and set aside.

Combine the butter and sugar in a large bowl and beat with an electric handheld mixer until pale and creamy. Add the eggs, one at a time, and continue to beat.

Next, add the chopped walnuts and mashed banana and fold in. Sift the flour, baking soda (bicarbonate of soda), baking powder, and salt over the mixture and gently fold all the ingredients together.

Spoon the batter into the buttered cake pan and use the back of a spoon to smooth the surface evenly. Bake for 35–40 minutes, or until a toothpick (skewer) inserted into the middle comes out clean. Let cool in the pan for 10 minutes, then turn out and let cool completely on a wire rack. Dust with confectioners' (icing) sugar, if using.

Ⓖ Replace the flour with a gluten-free alternative.

2 teaspoons anise seeds

1 cup (12 oz/350 g)
carob molasses

1 teaspoon baking
powder

2 pieces preserved
(stem) ginger, chopped

scant 1 cup (7 fl oz/
200 ml) sunflower oil

2 ⅓ cups (11 oz/300 g)
all-purpose (plain) flour

1 tablespoon sesame
seeds

Carob molasses and anise cake

A rich caramel cake that makes any kitchen smell wonderful. Sweet anise seeds, rich carob molasses, and crunchy sesame combine for a sophisticated sponge you will want to make time and time again.

Preparation time: 15 minutes
Cooking time: 45 minutes
Makes 1 (8-inch/20-cm) cake

Preheat the oven to 350°F/180°C/Gas Mark 4 and line an 8-inch/20-cm cake pan with parchment (baking) paper.

Pour 1 ½ cups (12 fl oz/350 ml) water into a saucepan and add the anise seeds. Bring to a boil and simmer for a minute. Strain into a small bowl and let cool, discarding the anise seeds.

Stir the carob molasses with the baking powder in a mixing bowl and let stand for a few minutes. Add the preserved (stem) ginger and then gradually stir in the sunflower oil and 1 ¼ cups (10 fl oz/300 ml) of infused anise water. Mix well.

Sift in the flour and whisk until incorporated. Pour the batter into the prepared cake pan and sprinkle on the sesame seeds.

Bake for 45 minutes. Let cool in the pan, then slice and serve.

Orange, plum, and almond cake

I like a slice or two of this with a cup of spiced tea. It takes a little while to prepare, but is well worth the effort.

Preparation time: 20 minutes
Cooking time: 120 minutes
Makes 1 (8-inch/20-cm) cake

Ⓖ

1 orange, peeled

butter, for greasing

½ cup (2 oz/100 g) superfine (caster) sugar

3 eggs, separated

⅓ cup (2 ½ oz/125 g) agave sugar

2 cups (7 oz/200 g) almond meal (ground almonds)

1 teaspoon gluten-free baking powder

3 plums, halved, pitted, and quartered

Put the orange into a saucepan and pour in enough water to cover. Bring to a boil, cover with a lid, reduce the heat, and simmer for 1½ hours (to speed this up, put it in a microwavable bowl with a scant ½ cup (3 ½ fl oz/100 ml) water, cover, and cook for 10–12 minutes on high (based on a 900W microwave). Drain the water from the pan.

Preheat the oven to 325°F/160°C/Gas Mark 3 and line the bottom of an 8-inch/20-cm loose-bottom cake pan with parchment (baking) paper.

Put the cooked orange and superfine (caster) sugar into a food processor and process to a puree.

Combine the egg yolks and agave sugar in a large mixing bowl and whisk until pale and creamy. Add the orange puree, almond meal (ground almonds), and baking powder and fold all the ingredients together.

Whisk the egg whites with an electric handheld mixer until soft peaks form. Fold into the orange mixture, one spoon at a time, until incorporated.

Pour the batter into the prepared cake pan. Arrange the plum quarters in the batter, pressing them in well. Bake for 40–50 minutes, or until a toothpick (skewer) inserted into the center comes out clean.

Remove from the oven and let cool in the pan on a wire rack. Remove the cake from the pan and peel off the parchment paper before slicing.

FOR THE CAKE

1 tablespoon Tahini
(page 24), for greasing

2 ½ cups (12 oz/350 g)
semolina flour (finely
ground semolina)

½ cup (3 ½ oz/100 g)
superfine (caster) sugar

1 teaspoon baking
powder

1 teaspoon baking soda
(bicarbonate of soda)

½ cup (4 fl oz/120 ml)
milk of your choice

½ cup (4 fl oz/120 ml)
plain (natural) yogurt

7 tablespoons (3 ½ oz/
100 g) unsalted butter,
melted

⅓ cup (2 oz/50 g)
blanched whole
almonds

FOR THE SYRUP

scant ⅔ cup (4 oz/120 g)
superfine (caster) sugar

juice of 1–2 lemons

1 lemon leaf

1 teaspoon rosewater

Almond semolina cake

We use a lot of semolina in Middle Eastern baking, mainly because of its beautiful crumbly texture. The flavors from the almonds and rosewater complement each other to make the cake sweet without being sickly.

Preparation time: 15 minutes
Cooking time: 40 minutes
Makes: 1 (8-inch/20-cm) square cake

Preheat the oven to 350°F/180°C/Gas Mark 4 and grease an 8-inch/20-cm square cake pan with the tahini.

Put all the dry ingredients for the cake into a stand mixer and beat together. Add the milk, yogurt, and melted butter and whisk to a creamy batter.

Pour the batter into the prepared cake pan and then arrange the almonds in a grid pattern on the surface so that when sliced each piece will have an almond on top. Bake for 40 minutes.

While the cake is baking, make the syrup by putting all the ingredients into a saucepan with ½ cup (4 fl oz/120 ml) water. Let the sugar dissolve over medium heat, then turn up the heat and boil to a syrupy consistency. Remove from the heat and let cool slightly.

When the cake is cooked, poke holes all over with a toothpick (skewer) and pour the syrup over the top. Let stand in the pan to absorb the syrup before serving.

Ⓥ Ⓖ

¾ cup (4 oz/120 g) rice
flour (ground rice)

1 teaspoon ground
cinnamon

2 teaspoons ground star
anise

2 teaspoons ground
caraway seeds

½ cup (3 ½ oz/100 g)
granulated sugar

2 teaspoons rosewater

pistachios, pine nuts,
flaked almonds, and
desiccated coconut, to
serve

Meghli

Traditionally, this Lebanese rice pudding is made to celebrate the birth of a baby and served to all friends and family visiting the newborn in the first few days of his or her life. I can remember making it when my brothers and sisters were born. It is also often served on Christmas Eve to celebrate the birth of Christ.

Preparation time: 10 minutes + 2 hours resting and 2 hours chilling time
Cooking time: 40 minutes
Serves: 6

Measure out 1 ⅔ cups (14 fl oz/400 ml) cold water in a large bowl, add the flour and stir well. Set aside for 2 hours.

Pour 4 ¼ cups (1 ¾ pints/1 liter) water into a large saucepan and bring to a boil over high heat. Carefully pour the flour-water mixture into the boiling water and stir well with a wooden spoon.

Reduce the heat to medium and gradually add the spices and sugar, stirring often, to prevent the mixture from sticking. Cook for 25–30 minutes, stirring frequently, until it thickens. Add the rosewater and mix well.

Use a ladle to divide the mixture between 6 small coffee cups or glasses. Sprinkle the pistachios, pine nuts, coconut, and flaked almonds on the top of each one.

Set aside to cool and then chill in the refrigerator for 2 hours, or until set, before serving.

Index